Plessy v. Ferguson:
separate but unequal

SUPREME COURT MILESTONES

Plessy v. Ferguson:

separate but unequal

JOAN AXELROD-CONTRADA

Marshall Cavendish
Benchmark

New York

With special thanks to Professor David M. O'Brien of the Woodrow Wilson Department of Politics at the University of Virginia for reviewing the text of this book.

Marshall Cavendish Benchmark
99 White Plains Road
Tarrytown, NY 10591
www.marshallcavendish.us

All Internet sites were available and accurate when sent to press.

Library of Congress Cataloging-in-Publication Data

Axelrod-Contrada, Joan.
   Plessy v. Ferguson : separate but unequal / by Joan Axelrod-Contrada.
       p. cm. — (Supreme Court milestones)
   Includes bibliographical references and index.
   ISBN 978-0-7614-2951-7
1. Plessy, Homer Adolph—Trials, litigation, etc.   2. Segregation in transportation—Law and legislation—Louisiana—History.
3. Segregation—Law and legislation—United States—History.   4. United States—Race relations—History.   I. Title.
KF223.P56A964 2009
342.7308′73—dc22
2007031606

Photo research by Connie Gardner

Cover photo by Williams Research Center/The Historic New Orleans Collection

The photographs in this book are used by permission and through the courtesy of:
Williams Research Center/The Historic New Orleans Collection: 1, 2-3, 42; *Corbis*: 6, 33, 80-81; Smithsonian Institution, 73; Frances Benjamin Johnston, 78, 85; Bettmann, 101; *The Granger Collection*: 10, 104, 109, 114; *Getty Images*: Hulton Archive, 14, 47, 48, 86; Bill Greenblatt, 26; *Art Resource*: Schomburg Center 28, 68; *AP Photo*: Ted S. Warren, 121.

Publisher: Michelle Bisson
Art Director: Anahid Hamparian
Series Designer: Sonia Chagbatzanian

Printed in Malaysia
1 3 5 6 4 2

contents

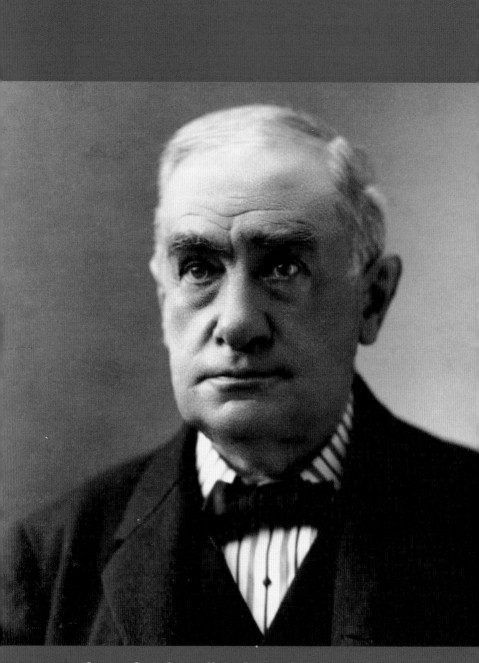

Supreme Court Justice Henry Billings Brown issued the majority decision in *Plessy* v. *Ferguson*, allowing separate but equal accommodations. He argued that overturning social inequalities was beyond the scope of the government.

introduction
The Journey of
"Separate but Equal"

In 1896, the supreme court's landmark decision in *Plessy* v. *Ferguson* legalized racial segregation, making "separate but equal" facilities the law of the land. The case began after Homer Plessy, a young shoemaker and member of the thriving Creole community in New Orleans, refused to leave his seat in the "whites only" train. Plessy, who was seven-eighths white and one-eighth black, could easily pass as white, thus exemplifying the ambiguities of race. Plessy was arrested for violating Louisiana's Separate Car Act.

Civil rights activists who arranged for Plessy's test case faced an uphill battle in a nation in which views of white supremacy had been passed down for generations. For many whites, segregation, particularly in the schools, seemed like a sensible way to reduce interracial conflict.

The case of *Plessy* v. *Ferguson* raised the question of whether or not the Thirteenth and Fourteenth Amendments, which were ratified after the Civil War, protected African Americans from segregation laws passed by the states. Justice Henry Billings Brown, who wrote the decision for the majority in *Plessy* v. *Ferguson*, argued that it was not the job of the federal government to correct social inequities. Justice Brown maintained that "in the nature of things," the Fourteenth Amendment "could not have been intended to abolish distinctions based upon color, or to enforce social, as distinguished from political, equality, or a commingling of the two races upon terms unsatisfactory to either."

Justice John Marshall Harlan issued a powerful dissent. The lone voice against the majority, Justice Harlan used the memorable metaphor of color blindness to maintain that all citizens were equal before the law. "Our constitution is color-blind, and neither knows nor tolerates classes among citizens," he declared.

He warned that segregation would fuel African-American resentments. "The destinies of the two races of this country are indissolubly linked together, and the interests of both require that the common government of all shall not permit the seeds of race hate to be planted under the sanction of the law," he wrote.

Nevertheless, Jim Crow (a term for segregation named after a character in a minstrel show) became the law of the land. Signs stating WHITES ONLY and COLORED marked virtually every aspect of life in the American South for more than the next half century. In 1954, the Supreme Court's historic decision in *Brown* v. *Board of Education* overturned *Plessy* v. *Ferguson*. Chief Justice Earl Warren put an end to "separate but equal" by declaring that "separate educational facilities are inherently unequal."

While *Brown* v. *Board of Education* outlawed legally mandated segregation in education, it did not erase the race line in America. Desegregation often gave way to resegregation. "One of the hard truths is that people are more comfortable around other people who are like them," said Sandra Robbie, author of a book about a Mexican-American desegregation case that paved the way for *Brown* v. *Board of Education*. "So it takes a conscious effort for people to build a bridge and learn about others."

Indeed, some questions raised by *Plessy* v. *Ferguson* are still being debated more than one hundred years later. In 1896, Justice Harlan's famous dissent declared that the Constitution was "color-blind." In 2007, the question of color blindness came before the Supreme Court in a case involving school diversity programs. Ironically, while the consideration of race was used by conservatives in 1896 to promote segregation, liberals on the Supreme Court in 2007 argued for race-conscious policies to protect diversity. Such debates show that the issues raised by *Plessy* v. *Ferguson* remain with us today.

It wasn't until 1954 that "separate but equal" facilities were made illegal. This 1856 engraving depicts a conductor expelling a free person of color from a railroad car reserved for white people.

one
EJECTED FROM THE TRAIN

ON JUNE 7, 1892, HOMER PLESSY arrived at the train station in New Orleans for his date with history. The weather that day was typical for New Orleans: hot and steamy. Despite the warm temperatures, the twenty-nine-year-old shoemaker wore a suit and hat, the attire of a passenger riding in first class.

Plessy walked by the signs that said COLORED. His complexion was so light, he could easily be called white. He went up to the window and asked for a first-class ticket to Covington, a town about 30 miles (48 km) north of New Orleans. Travelers could see the Mississippi River just behind the depot.

The clerk gave Plessy his ticket without question. The train for Covington was scheduled to leave at 4:15 p.m.

Right on time, the whistle blew. Steam spewed from the engine. The doors opened, and Plessy took his place on the train.

"I have to tell you that, according to Louisiana law, I am a colored man," Plessy told the conductor, J. J. Dowling, as he handed him the ticket.

"Then you will have to retire to the colored car," Dowling told him. The colored coach was also known as the Jim Crow car, a term derived from an old minstrel show in which whites darkened their faces to poke fun at blacks. Ash from the train's engine spilled into the Jim Crow car,

WHO was JIm Crow?

Whether or not Jim Crow was a real person is impossible to say. The legend is that white entertainer Thomas "Daddy" Rice saw a small black boy (or, some say, an elderly black man) dancing and singing a song called "Jump Jim Crow." Sometime around 1830, Rice blackened his face with charcoal paste or burnt cork and incorporated the character of Jim Crow into his minstrel show. His depiction of a happy, strutting, ignorant black man played to white stereotypes of African Americans. *Jim Crow* became a derogatory synonym for Negro. When states began legislating formal codes to keep blacks and whites apart, Jim Crow served as a label for such laws.

which had wooden benches instead of the upholstered seats of the first-class coach.

Plessy told Dowling as the train pulled out of the station that he had paid for a first-class ticket and intended to stay put. Dowling recruited the help of officer Chris Cain, a private detective.

"If you are colored, you should go into the car set apart for your race," said Cain. "The law is plain and must be obeyed."

Once again, Plessy refused, saying he would rather go to jail than abandon the coach. Cain told the shoemaker to come with him. Without further argument, Plessy accompanied Cain to the police station on Elysian Fields Avenue, where he was booked for violating the 1890 Separate Car Act. The law called for "equal but separate" accommodations for "white" and "colored" passengers. The penalty for violating the law was a twenty-five-dollar fine or twenty days in jail.

NO ACT OF Happenstance

Plessy's act of civil disobedience was no act of happenstance. Instead, it was a carefully orchestrated plan developed by a committee of activists to test the constitutionality of Louisiana's Separate Car Act. The organizers chose Plessy to board the train because they believed his light complexion would highlight the difficulty of classifying people by race. Plessy was only one-eighth black. The organizers gave Plessy careful instructions to carry out a four-part plan:

Get the ticket.

Board the train.

Get arrested.

Get booked.

Plessy carried out the plan perfectly, but he was not one to seek the spotlight. Historians know little about Plessy the man. He left behind no photographs or personal writings. Public records, though, show that he took part in civic organizations and lived with his wife, Louise, in a racially integrated, middle-class neighborhood in New Orleans not far from where jazz legend Louis Armstrong would later blow his horn. One of Plessy's twenty-first-century relatives described him as a "relatively quiet, ordinary citizen who got involved, and, beyond that, there were no other events in his life that would have marked him for history."

TWO Fiery Leaders

Two fiery leaders laid the groundwork for Plessy's historic ride: forty-three-year-old newspaper editor Louis Martinet and fifty-four-year-old lawyer/novelist Albion Tourgée. The two were kindred spirits, both uncompromising idealists who combined writing with activism. Martinet, who was of mixed race, edited the radical weekly the *Crusader* from his offices in the French Quarter.

ALBION TOURGÉE SCHEMED WITH LOUIS MARTINET TO UNDERMINE THE SEPARATE CAR ACT. DESPITE THEIR HARD WORK, WHICH PUT TOURGÉE'S FAMILY IN FINANCIAL TROUBLE, THEY FAILED IN THEIR ATTEMPT. THE SUPREME COURT SAID SEGREGATION WAS NEITHER UNCONSTITUTIONAL NOR A FEDERAL ISSUE.

Tourgée was a famous novelist, lawyer, judge, and perhaps the nation's leading white proponent of racial equality. He had heard about opposition to the Separate Car Act from a black Kansan who had visited New Orleans. Tourgée, who lived in Mayfield, New York, coordinated their legal strategy with Martinet by mail.

The two men admired each other. Tourgée considered Martinet a hero for protesting against segregation from inside the Deep South. Martinet, in turn, admired Tourgée's efforts to advocate for racial equality on the national stage. "You are fighting a great battle, Judge," Martinet wrote. "You are, if not the only one, the foremost militant apostle of liberty in the whole land."

ALBION TOURGÉE:
A LIFE LIKE A NOVEL

Albion Tourgée made his mark on the world not only as the lead lawyer in *Plessy* v. *Ferguson* but also as a best-selling novelist.

Tourgée, who resembled the colorful, stubborn, and idealistic characters of his novels, developed his characteristically rebellious and egalitarian spirit early in life. Born in Williamsfield, Ohio, on May 2, 1838, he grew up on a family farm on the American frontier. His mother, Louisa Winegar Tourgée, died when he was five, after which his father, Valentine Tourgée, remarried. Young Albion asserted his independence by stalking off into the woods with his father's hunting rifle and surviving on small game until he felt like coming home. His father, who had grown increasingly religious and authoritarian, burned books he decided were immoral for his son to read. At the age of thirteen, Tourgée went to live with his maternal uncle in Lee, Massachusetts.

Two years later, he returned to Ohio. Considered handsome, with blue eyes, sculpted features, and a lanky frame, Tourgée worked odd jobs to pay the tuition at Kingsville Academy, a private school. At Kingsville, he met Emma Kilbourne, whose steady and practical nature provided the perfect balance to his own impulsive and emotional temperament. He told Emma that he had always felt himself "an orphan in spirit."

Before marrying Emma, Tourgée attended the University of Rochester and joined the Union army. During the Civil War, he got in trouble with his superior officers for insubordination, was severely injured three times, and spent four months in a Confederate prison. In captivity, he studied Spanish and read *Don Quixote*, the tale of an idealist's quest for the impossible dream.

After the war, Tourgée studied law and decided that he and Emma should move to the South. The next fourteen years in North Carolina would be extremely rocky ones for Tourgée. As an outspoken advocate of racial equality, he clashed with politicians and townspeople. He set out to run a nursery garden, but the business failed, as did his next venture, a factory for making tool handles. A string of political failures followed, including four unsuccessful bids for seats in the U.S. Congress. Nevertheless, Tourgée obtained some measure of public success. In 1868, he was elected judge of the state superior court.

From his seat on the bench, Tourgée denounced the crimes of the Ku Klux Klan and other white supremacists. He also established a radical newspaper, which prompted comments such as "Go back home you . . . Yankee & stay there." Despite threats on his life, Tourgée kept up his attacks, riding his old horse from meeting to meeting and carrying a pistol for protection. One conservative Democrat threatened to shoot him, but Tourgée won the standoff by staring down his opponent. The governor of North Carolina called him "the meanest Yankee who has ever settled among us." Finally, after the Ku Klux Klan showed up at his house one night, Tourgée decided to move his family to upstate New York.

A man of extreme highs and lows, he became depressed after the nation turned its back on Reconstruction. After one sleepless night in 1877, Tourgée rose with new clarity and told Emma, "I am going to write a book and call it *A Fool's Errand.*" The book would be an autobiographical account of a Northerner's experiences in the South during Reconstruction. Tourgée worked feverishly on the book, which was published anonymously in 1879 as *A Fool's Errand By One of the Fools*.

A Fool's Errand became an instant hit, with reviewers comparing it to Harriet Beecher Stowe's *Uncle Tom's Cabin* and Charles Dickens's *A Tale of Two Cities*. Tourgée portrayed the North and South as two separate countries. While agreeing with the views of the North, he felt sympathy for the proud and defiant people of the South: "One can not help but admire the arrogant boldness with which they charged the nation which had overpowered them," he wrote. The book's anonymous authorship added to its allure.

Once Tourgée revealed his identity in the second edition, prominent people sought him out. At the 1880 Republican convention, delegates pledged their support for the type of national education system he advocated in *A Fool's Errand*. Tourgée stumped for presidential candidate James Garfield, a childhood friend from Ohio. Upon winning the election, Garfield summoned his old friend to the White House and asked him to write a book about national education policy. The president expressed his hope that America would be a "paradise for all such fools."

However, after less than a year in office, Garfield was assassinated by a former supporter who had been passed over for federal patronage. As the nation's interest in the problems of Reconstruction began to wane, so too did Tourgée's mainstream popularity. His books and columns (he wrote more than twenty books altogether) appealed mostly to a dwindling number of like-minded people such as those involved in the case against the Separate Car Act in Louisiana.

Despite his family's desperate financial circumstances, Tourgée refused to take any payment for his work on *Plessy* v. *Ferguson*. "His mind was too large to take in business details," Emma once lamented. Tourgée knew his chances of winning *Plessy* v. *Ferguson* were slim. However, he won over at least one member of the Supreme Court with his memorable line: "Justice is pictured blind and her daughter, the Law, ought at least to be color-blind."

After the verdict, Tourgée took a consulate position in Bordeaux, France, where his brash sensibilities once again irritated his superiors. In one instance, he irreverently referred to America's low-grade apples as containing "inhabitants," meaning worms. During his years abroad, Tourgée maintained his interest in race relations back home. In 1901, he congratulated President Theodore Roosevelt for inviting a black man, Booker T. Washington, to the White House. On May 21, 1905, Albion Tourgée died, completing his "Fool's Errand" on earth but leaving behind a body of idealistic works.

Martinet was a proud, neatly dressed man known for wearing a black string tie and wide-brimmed felt hat. A lawyer and physician as well as a journalist, he refused to play the part of the subservient Negro. Even in the face of danger, he refused to be cowed, as he told Tourgée in a letter:

> I believe I remain the only active politician who was not, at one time or another, driven from the parish through fear and intimidation. I was often threatened & several times saw guns leveled at me. But I never flinched & always maintained my ground & used to carry openly an arsenal about me.

As the local organizer, Martinet hired private detective Cain and won the cooperation of the railroad company. The railroad secretly objected to the Separate Car Act because it created additional expenses for them, requiring them to run extra cars, but they kept their opposition quiet to stay in the good graces of conservative whites. Some railroads posted the signs WHITE and COLORED but let passengers go wherever they pleased.

Martinet also took steps to ensure Plessy's safety. He wanted to avoid the possibility that people on the train would "simply beat & throw him out & [that] there [would] be no arrest." To avoid violence, Martinet arranged with the railroad for the arrest to occur before the train started.

Free People of Color

Martinet personified New Orleans' thriving population of free people of color, also called black Creoles. This group included the offspring of French settlers and women of color, either slave or free, as well as free blacks from other French colonies in the West Indies, such as Haiti and Martinique. Originally a French, then Spanish, then once again French colony, Louisiana became part of the United States in 1803, when Thomas Jefferson purchased it from France. At the time of Plessy's historic train ride, many members of the Creole community in New Orleans still spoke French.

Many creoles considered themselves to be members of a third race rather than white or black. The free people of color of New Orleans lived in a world of contradictions. On the one hand, they differed from slaves in their high level of economic and professional success. On the other hand, they lacked the social and political rights of the white elite. One Louisiana law, for example, prohibited free persons of color from presuming themselves "equal to the white."

Still, a fair amount of mixing took place between the races. Early in its history, New Orleans gained a reputation as the South's good-time town, famous for its taverns, gambling halls, ballrooms, and bordellos. A shortage of white women on the frontier prompted white men to cross the racial divide for female companionship. Dances limited to white men and free black women drew large crowds, causing white women to grumble about being deprived of dance partners. People identified offspring of interracial liaisons by their percentage of white blood as follows:

> mulatto: the offspring of an interracial couple
> quadroon: having one black grandparent
> octoroon: having one black great-grandparent

Like its famous gumbo, the population of New Orleans brought together a mix of cultures. In one of his letters to Tourgée, Martinet described the racial ambiguity of the town:

> There are the strangest white people you ever saw here. Walking up and down our principal thoroughfare—Canal Street—you would [be] surprised

to have persons pointed out to you, some as white & others as colored, and if you were not informed you would be sure to pick out the white for colored and the colored for white. Besides people of tolerably fair complexion, even if unmistakably colored, enjoy here a large degree of immunity from the accursed prejudice.

Not surprisingly, many residents objected to being categorized as "white" or "colored." One man declared, "I cannot tell you if I am a white man or a colored man." He boasted that no one in his family had been a slave. With a hint of displeasure, he observed, "They call me in Louisiana a colored."

OPPOSING THE SEPARATE CAR ACT

When the Separate Car Act came before the Louisiana legislature in the spring of 1890, Martinet and a group of like-minded citizens protested the bill. In a statement, the group wrote:

We do not think that citizens of a darker hue should be treated by law on different lines than those of a lighter complexion. Citizenship is national and has no color. We hold that any attempt to abridge it on account of color is simply a surrender of wisdom to the appeals of passion.

Despite their opposition, the Separate Car Act passed the Louisiana Senate on July 9, 1890. That same day, Martinet sent an urgent telegram to Governor Francis T. Nicholls asking him to veto the measure. "Governor, thousands good and true men urge you to veto Separate Car Act." Despite Martinet's plea, Governor Nicholls signed the act into law on July 10, 1890.

At first, Martinet's *Crusader* called for a boycott of the trains. However, since few citizens believed their actions would make a difference, the boycott failed. In the pages of the *Crusader*, Martinet called for a new strategy: "We'll make a case, a test case, and bring it before the Federal Courts on the grounds of the invasion of the right [of] a person to travel through the States unmolested."

Martinet and his allies formed a new organization, the Citizens' Committee to Test the Constitutionality of the Separate Car Act. They raised money from rich and poor alike to challenge the law. After Tourgée offered to represent the group for free, the Citizens' Committee decided to hire a local white attorney, James Walker, to assist him.

Martinet described Walker as "a friend & a conscientious & painstaking lawyer."

Tourgée and Walker began planning their legal strategy by mail. However, their first test case got off to a bumpy start. Homer Plessy wasn't the original volunteer chosen to challenge the Separate Car Act.

FIrST TrY

Initially, the Citizens' Committee decided to target an interstate train to challenge the Separate Car Act's authority over trains traveling out of state. The Interstate Commerce Act applied to businesses that crossed state lines, including railroads. Tourgée and Walker planned to argue that the Separate Car Act unfairly hampered commerce by requiring railroads to run additional cars.

In addition, the group wanted to focus attention on the ambiguity of race. How would a conductor know how to identify a passenger by race? What if someone were misidentified? Would the railroad be held liable? Such questions would be particularly difficult to answer in the case of passengers of mixed race, Tourgée believed.

Not everyone, however, applauded his strategy. In New

Orleans, a black minister named Alexander S. Jackson accused the Citizens' Committee of representing the interest of only those who were nearly white or wanted to pass as white. Martinet dismissed Jackson's accusations as "absurd and malicious" and "a lot of nonsense." At least one prominent member of the Citizens' Committee had dark skin.

Meanwhile, Martinet worked behind the scenes to set up the test ride. Officials at the first railroad he approached told him they did not enforce the law. Next, he approached officials at the Louisville and Nashville Railroad. The officials agreed to the test case as long as no publicity pointed to them.

The Citizens' Committee chose twenty-one-year-old Daniel Desdunes, the light-skinned son of the prominent committee member Rodolphe Desdunes, to ride the train. Like Plessy, Desdunes was one-eighth black.

On February 24, 1892, Daniel Desdunes purchased a first-class ticket for a trip from New Orleans to Mobile, Alabama. When Desdunes boarded the train, he ignored officials who directed him to the coach for colored passengers. Instead, he took a place on the first-class coach. A complaint was issued against him, and he was charged with violating the Separate Car Act.

While the Citizens' Committee waited for a hearing on the charges against Daniel Desdunes, another case involving the railroads came before the Louisiana Supreme Court. In the case of *Abbott* v. *Hicks*, a conductor working for the Texas and Pacific Railway was charged with admitting a black passenger to a white car. The lawyer for the conductor argued that the Separate Car Act was invalid because it had allowed a state law to supersede the federal government's authority over interstate commerce.

The Louisiana Supreme Court agreed that the Separate Car Act was unconstitutional on interstate trains. As a result of the ruling, the case against Desdunes was dismissed.

At first, Martinet viewed the verdict as a victory. "Jim Crow is dead as a door nail," he proclaimed. However, Jim Crow was still very much alive on trains traveling within the state—hence the need for another test case. This time, the group would choose a train that stayed within the borders of Louisiana.

SECOND TRY

Once again, Martinet worked behind the scenes to set up the ride. This time, the committee settled on Homer Plessy, a friend of Rodolphe Desdunes's, to challenge the law. Plessy followed the committee's script to the letter. The committee's careful planning kept his ride brief, so his risk of attack by white vigilantes would be low.

Everything went according to plan. Committee members met Plessy at the police station. Paul Bonseigneur, the group's treasurer, offered his house as security to pay for Plessy's bail. Plessy would be arraigned the following day. Unlike most lawyers, Tourgée and Walker wanted a guilty verdict for their client. Such a verdict would allow them to appeal the decision to the next level. They wanted to bring their case all the way to the U.S. Supreme Court.

TWO

BACKING UP: THE HISTORY OF SEGREGATION

America laid down tracks for the separation of the races early on. Despite the lofty words in the Declaration of Independence that "all men are created equal," the U.S. Constitution counted each slave as only three-fifths of a person. The system of race-based slavery took root because whites regarded blacks as inferior. Slaveholders, though, were not the only ones who held such prejudices. In 1841, Massachusetts, a hotbed of abolitionist sentiment, became the first state in the nation to pass a law requiring railroads to provide separate cars for blacks.

"One of the strangest things about the career of Jim Crow," wrote historian C. Vann Woodward, "was that the system was born in the North and reached an advanced age before moving South in force." Although many people have associated segregation with the South, it began in the North.

In the middle of the nineteenth century, conflicts about slavery became so intense, the United States came close to splitting in two. On March 6, 1857, the Supreme Court's controversial decision in the *Dred Scott* case fueled the tensions between North and South. In a 7 to 2 decision, the Court ruled against Dred Scott, who had sued his

In 1846, Dred Scott and his wife Harriet filed suit for their freedom in the St. Louis Circuit Court. This suit began an eleven-year legal fight that ended in the U.S. Supreme Court, which issued a landmark decision declaring that Scott remain a slave. This decision contributed to rising tensions between the free and slave states just before the American Civil War.

The records displayed in this exhibit document the Scotts' early struggle to gain their freedom through litigation and are the only extant records of this significant case as it was heard in the St. Louis Circuit Court.

IN 1846, DRED AND HARRIET SCOTT SUED FOR THEIR FREEDOM FROM SLAVERY IN THE ST. LOUIS CIRCUIT COURT, STARTING A BATTLE THAT WOULD END IN DEFEAT IN THE U.S. SUPREME COURT ELEVEN YEARS LATER. THAT DECISION SET A PRECEDENT FOR *PLESSY*.

master for his freedom. Chief Justice Roger B. Taney declared that slaves could not be citizens because they had "no rights which the white man was bound to respect." In 1861, the Civil War erupted.

born in tumultuous times
Homer Plessy was born during these tumultuous times, on March 17, 1863, in New Orleans. The Civil War stood at its halfway point. Union forces occupied the cosmopolitan city of New Orleans, which was widely known for its large

26

population of free people of color, often called Creoles because of their French ancestry. This group consisted of former slaves (French tradition called for a slaveholder to free his slaves shortly before his own death), immigrants from such islands as Haiti in the West Indies, and offspring of mixed races. Members of this highly accomplished group took pride in their French-speaking culture and status as nonslaves, refusing to think of themselves as subordinate to whites. As Louisiana historian Charles Gayarre put it, "They walked erect."

In New Orleans, racial mixing and segregation had long existed side by side. On the one hand, people of all races and ethnic groups lived together in New Orleans' downtown neighborhoods. Some upper-class whites hired free black men to teach their daughters music. Whites and blacks also mixed freely in the back-alley taverns, dance halls, gambling joints, and bordellos.

On the other hand, whites relegated blacks to separate streetcars, trains, restaurants, and inns. The famous New Orleans Opera House set aside a section of boxes in the upper gallery for the African-American elite.

During the Civil War, new calls sounded for racial equality. In particular, the free people of color wanted to end segregation on the city's mule-powered streetcars. New Orleans still used animals for transportation in the downtown district because of objections to the noise and soot locomotives would create. About a third of the mule-drawn streetcars bore large black stars, marking them as "star cars" for African-American passengers. In 1863, a delegation of mixed-race Creoles persuaded the Union army to integrate the streetcars. However, a court decision reversed the order.

Segregation persisted even after the Union army won the Civil War, in 1865. Southern legislatures passed the infamous Black Codes, restricting the freedom of African

Americans. Train conductors habitually directed African Americans to the dingy coach just behind the engine, known as the "smoking car."

streetcar victory

Finally, in the spring of 1867, a mass protest erupted over segregation on the streetcars. One protester grabbed the reins from a driver and drove off with a formerly white car like a trophy of war. During the weekend of May 4–5, 1867, crowds of blacks boarded cars previously reserved for whites. When a driver told one black man to get off, the crowd chanted, "Stay on. Stay on." Riots broke out. The

Ladies' Cars

Ida B. Wells considered herself a lady.

But no matter how refined, educated, and well dressed a black woman might be, few nineteenth-century white Americans afforded her the privileges she would receive if she were white. When Wells, a twenty-two-year-old African-American schoolteacher with fashionably upswept hair, took her place in the ladies' car one day in May 1884, the conductor told her she needed to move to the smoking car, which served as the second-class coach. Wells refused to budge, so the conductor got two burly men to help him lift her from her seat and drag her down to the smoking car, where men drank, smoked, gambled, and used foul language. Whites, scoffing at the idea of a black woman who "played the lady," cheered her removal.

In the Victorian world of the mid–1800s, railroads adhered to the etiquette of the day, which protected ladies from the rougher influence of the opposite sex. The genders had become more separate as men left the family farm for jobs in industry. Etiquette books described how the men and women were to behave in public. Because the era celebrated women's "natural" sphere of home and family, railroads tried to make the ladies' cars resemble homes away from home. On the trains, gentlemen were expected to give up their seats, help female passengers with their bags, open windows for them, and bring them refreshments. In return for this deference, female travelers were supposed to be gracious but not overly flirtatious.

Middle-class black women such as Ida B. Wells adhered to the same rules of etiquette as their white counterparts, assuming that, if they carried themselves like ladies, they too could claim the privileges of gender. A long history of sexual exploitation by white men had made many black women fearful of the rough-and-tumble atmosphere of the smoking car, where they encountered everything from obscene comments to physical attacks. As a black woman named Mary Church Terrell recalled in the 1880s, "I had heard about awful tragedies which had overtaken colored girls who had been obliged to travel in these cars at night."

After getting off the train as soon as she could, Wells sued for being unjustly removed from the ladies' car. Surprisingly, she won. A Minnesota-born judge ordered the Chesapeake and Ohio Railroad to pay Wells five hundred dollars in damages. The decision created a stir. DARKY DAMSEL GETS DAMAGES, blared one headline. An upper court, however, reversed the decision, ordering Wells to pay two hundred dollars in court costs. Wells went on to become a journalist and well-known advocate for her race.

From the start, the ladies' car was a flexible system, allowing for the inclusion of some men. Many women traveled with family members or husbands (for example, on their honeymoon) by train. Because men accompanying women could sit in the ladies' car, some males traveling alone pretended to have a female companion to get a seat on the first-class train. In one case, a man who helped a female stranger with her bags claimed she was "his lady."

In the 1860s and 1870s, men became increasingly disgruntled over their lack of privileges on the train. Why should they have to surrender their seats? After all, not all women acted like ladies. Some female passengers rudely expected men to give up their seats without so much as a thank you. Moreover, not all men who accompanied women acted like gentlemen. As one male traveler put it, "Because an inveterate chewer and squirter of tobacco has his wife with him, it does not follow that he should have a better right to the ladies' car than a well-bred gentleman who traveled singly."

One man, unhappy with standing in the smoking car without a seat, attempted to enter the ladies' car but was forcibly removed upon arrival. In response, he brought suit against the railroad. In the 1874 case of *Bass* v. *Chicago & Northwestern Railway Company*, the Supreme Court of Wisconsin decided in favor of the railroad's right to create separate accommodations for women, stating

> In view of the crowds of men of all sorts. . . . It appears to us to be not only a reasonable regulation, but almost if not quite a humane duty, for the railroad companies to appropriate a car of each passenger train primarily for women and men accompanying them.

Nevertheless, as the nineteenth century wore on, the railroads took new pains to cater to the needs and tastes of male travelers. For white men, the ability to pay for a first-class ticket increasingly took precedence over the demands of chivalry. Railroads began providing special luxuries such as smoking saloons, barber shops, and writing desks for gentlemen.

With the rise of Jim Crow in the 1880s and 1890s, black women lost their ability to claim gender over race as the grounds for a first-class ticket. Ironically, courts pointed to the ladies' cars, which so many black women had fought to enter, as justification for racial segregation on the railroads. If the railroads could provide separate cars for ladies, then they could also set aside some cars for "white" and others for "colored" travelers.

In the twenty-first century, a new type of ladies' car came on the scene. A few major cities around the world established women-only cars to protect female travelers from male "gropers" on crowded rush-hour trains. In Rio de Janeiro, Brazil, for instance, pink stripes on windows and doors adorn the women-only cars. In Tokyo, Japan, many men who worry about being falsely accused of groping if they accidentally brush up against women support the female-only cars. Some men, however, grumble about being crowded into the remaining cars. Their sentiments echo those of men excluded from the ladies' cars in nineteenth-century America.

next day, streetcar companies realized they had no choice but to abolish the star car system.

African Americans followed up their streetcar victory by challenging the color line in restaurants, taverns, and soda shops throughout the city. They had learned that mass resistance could bring about change.

RADICAL RECONSTRUCTION: NEW FREEDOMS

Homer Plessy's childhood coincided with the era of Radical Reconstruction, a time of new freedoms for African Americans. The Reconstruction Acts of 1867 and 1868 divided the South into five military districts supported by federal troops. Congress approved three new amendments to the Constitution intended to reverse the Black Codes: the Thirteenth Amendment, which ended slavery; the Fourteenth Amendment, which guaranteed citizenship and equal protection under the law; and the Fifteenth Amendment, which gave blacks the right to vote. To be readmitted to the Union, Southern states needed to ratify the Fourteenth Amendment. In Louisiana, a new alliance of African Americans and white carpetbaggers

Pinckney Pinchback, the son of a white planter and a black slave,
briefly served as Louisiana's acting governor in 1872, and was even
elected to Congress but was never allowed to serve.

with a pro-integration agenda replaced the old order.
Many of the leaders hailed from the mixed-race Creole
community.

One by one, old segregation orders gave way to new
laws mandating equal rights. Louisiana's "black and tan"
constitution of 1868 outlawed racial segregation in public
schools and places of public accommodation. Another
provision of the constitution called for state officeholders
to accept "the civil and political equality of all men."

Not surprisingly, Louisiana's conservative press
blasted the new document. One newspaper accused the
constitution of "crimes against reason, against religion,

33

and against nature." Another denounced the constitution as "a condensed charter of all the turpitudes and monstrosities which negro depravity and fanatical partisanship are attempting to impose upon us."

But the white conservatives lacked the votes needed to defeat the constitution. On April 18, 1868, the new document became the law of Louisiana. For Homer Plessy, the following year brought a mixture of personal sorrow and political gains. Although his father, Adolphe, died in 1869, the Louisiana legislature passed a new civil rights act. Anyone who experienced discrimination in public accommodations could sue for damages. In 1871, a black sheriff named C. S. Sauvinet won a one-thousand-dollar settlement against a tavern that refused to serve him a drink. Also in 1871, Homer Plessy's mother, Rosa Debergue, married Victor Dupart, an idealistic Creole.

Great numbers of Creoles and freedmen won election to political office. On December 9, 1872, Lieutenant Governor P. B. S. Pinchback, an African American, became the acting governor of Louisiana (during impeachment proceedings against Governor Henry Clay Warmoth). The son of a white Mississippi planter and a female slave, Pinchback had come to New Orleans as a cabin boy during the Civil War and had gotten involved in the Republican Party.

Political power gave blacks a new tool to use against railroad companies that customarily directed African Americans to the smoking car. The state's new multiracial legislature had the power to approve or revoke railroad charters. If a company failed to carry out a policy of nondiscrimination, the state could revoke its charter.

BACKLASH

Many white Southerners, meanwhile, regarded the years from 1868 to 1876 as the "tragic era." Confederate soldiers had returned home from the field of battle only to find their jobs taken over by African Americans they saw as inferior and white Northerners they despised as intruders. White Southerners derided the Northern newcomers, known as "carpetbaggers," who carried their possessions in suitcases made by stitching together two pieces of carpet. Among the most famous carpetbaggers was lawyer Albion Tourgée. During his years as a judge in North Carolina, Tourgée attracted the wrath of a new group of white supremacists who called themselves the Ku Klux Klan.

The Ku Klux Klan began as a social club for Confederate war veterans in 1865. When Klan members saw the terrifying effect their pointed hoods and long white robes had on black neighbors who believed in ghosts and other supernatural beings, the group took on a more intimidating stance. Klan members roamed the countryside, threatening, assaulting, and sometimes killing African Americans. Mob hangings were known as lynchings, after the eighteenth-century vigilante William Lynch.

Other whites used more subtle means to keep blacks down. They simply refused to serve African Americans in their restaurants, taverns, and soda shops despite the state's civil rights laws. Few African Americans had the money or the inclination to challenge the old customs of segregation.

A GILDED AGE

In 1873, the United States suffered a severe financial panic as a result of the economic strains of rapid growth. The panic caused by a shortage of currency gave way to a large-scale economic depression. In an era marked by the tremendous wealth of such big industrialists as Andrew Carnegie and John D. Rockefeller, unemployment and despair grew. The wealth of the nation was illusory—gold on the surface with lead underneath. Writer Mark Twain called it the "Gilded Age."

Reactions to the economic depression varied. While some whites lashed out at blacks in anger, in 1873 in Louisiana, others joined the Unification Movement for racial harmony. Homer Plessy's new stepfather, Victor Dupart, became involved in this movement. The alliance of blacks and whites, Christians and Jews, Republicans and Democrats succumbed within months to internal disagreements. Nevertheless, Homer Plessy probably heard talk at home about the exciting new possibilities of interracial cooperation.

On the national level, President Ulysses S. Grant signed into law the controversial Civil Rights Act on March 1, 1875. The law prohibited racial discrimination in public facilities, such as trains and restaurants. Violators could be fined as much as one thousand dollars, imprisoned for at least thirty days, and directed to pay the injured party five hundred dollars in damages.

In New Orleans, African Americans buoyed by the new law demanded service in restaurants and taverns. Some businesses welcomed the new customers while others devised ingenious ways to drive them away without overtly violating the law. They saturated the food of blacks with salt, pepper, or vinegar. One bartender served an African-American customer a soft drink doctored with cayenne pepper. The gasping customer tried to have the bartender arrested, but the policeman considered the dispute "entirely a matter of taste."

Whites also implemented poll taxes to keep African Americans from voting. Since most blacks were poor, they could not afford the new fees. In many locations, the tax kept new voters from returning to the polls.

reconstruction ends

At the age of fourteen, Homer Plessy once again saw history change course. The era of Radical Reconstruction

Tale of Terror

In 1885, an African-American teacher named Samuel E. Courtney learned about white vigilante justice the hard way—through personal experience. Courtney chronicled his hellish journey on an Alabama train in a Boston newspaper. Because he and his two fellow teachers were light-skinned blacks who could sometimes pass as white, they thought they could travel in the first-class train without any trouble. But they were wrong. When the train stopped for refreshments, a group of angry whites surrounded the train.

"There are three coons on that first-class car," one called out.

"Put 'em off," someone else said.

Then twelve white men carrying revolvers approached Courtney and his friends.

"Say, you look like an intelligent [racial epithet deleted]," one of the armed men told Courtney. "Don't you know better than to ride in a first-class car? Before we'll let you ride any further in that car, we'll take you out there in the field and fill you with bullets."

For the rest of the trip, Courtney and his friends rode in the Jim Crow car. When the train came to its next stop, they told the superintendent of the train about their harrowing experience. The superintendent arranged for a private car to take Courtney and his two friends to their destination.

On the way back, the group encountered more trouble, including fines for trumped-up offenses such as loitering commonly levied against African Americans. The three teachers made the final leg of their trip by horseback. "That night we drove thirty-five miles through the woods," Courtney wrote. It was the kind of experience a person would never forget.

ended when Southerners agreed to accept Republican Rutherford B. Hayes as president after the disputed election of 1876 in return for his withdrawal of federal troops from the South. The South went back to running its own affairs. If the Civil War and Reconstruction provided the backdrop for Plessy's youth, the aftermath shaped his development as a young man.

At first, the conservative white Southern Democrats, called Redeemers, seemed willing to protect at least some black rights. Governor Francis Nicholls of Louisiana, for instance, promised to "obliterate the color line in politics and to consolidate the people on the basis of equal rights and common interests."

During the 1870s and 1880s, segregation policies in the South were often inconsistent. One train conductor might let African Americans sit wherever they'd like while another might direct them to the Jim Crow car. Segregation did not yet have the force of law. As historian C. Vann Woodward observed, "It was a time of experiment, testing, and uncertainty."

For some whites, social class mattered more than race. They looked down on the unruly members of their own race who felt the need to humiliate blacks. "It is a great deal pleasanter to travel with respectable and well-behaved colored people than with unmannerly and ruffianly white men," a Charleston, South Carolina, newspaper writer remarked.

In 1879, Albion Tourgée published his autobiographical tale, *A Fool's Errand By One of the Fools*, which quickly became a best seller. The book cast both the federal government and the Ku Klux Klan in a bad light but offered hope that education would improve the lives of Southern blacks. Tourgée's book brought him much acclaim, including invitations to the White House.

Meanwhile, in Louisiana, Louis Martinet saw promise

in the moderate policies of Democratic governor Nicholls. Nicholls had appointed several African Americans to minor positions in his administration and opposed a measure to limit primaries to whites. Such policies set him apart from the party's traditional hard-liners. However, Nicholls' support of segregated schools disappointed many black leaders, including Martinet.

Racism Gains Ground

As the 1880s wore on, Martinet noticed a change in the political climate. In a letter to Tourgée, Martinet wrote about how the voices of moderation in the Democratic Party had become increasingly silenced by the demands of white racists. "Their cry was 'white supremacy all along the line,'" he wrote. As a result, Martinet left the Democratic Party in disgust.

Others, too, noticed a change. For some, segregation seemed like a sensible way to quell the violence of the times. By keeping the races apart, segregation fit right in with the progressive reforms aimed at enlightened public policy. Southern segregationists also got a boost from a change of heart in the North. The North's old preoccupation with the rights of the freedmen faded as other matters, such as the troubled economy, assumed new importance. At the same time, white Northerners developed more sympathy for their counterparts in the South as the migration of blacks to their region and an influx of immigrants from southern and eastern Europe raised new fears about the dilution of the "Anglo-Saxon racial stock."

In Congress, Republican legislators let economic issues such as tariffs and currency take priority over the protection of blacks' voting rights. Left to their own devices, Southern states passed new literacy tests that reduced the numbers of African-American voters.

Theoretically, the tests applied to whites as well as blacks, with supporters arguing that the nation needed a literate and well-informed electorate. However, in practice, election officials used the tests to discriminate against blacks. Election officials could pass all white voters and reject all black voters without having to justify their decisions. Voting fraud and intimidation also kept many African Americans away from the polls. Those who attempted to vote risked violence from white supremacist groups, such as the Ku Klux Klan.

Sidelined from the political process, some African Americans decided to emigrate to Africa or settle in the more welcoming state of Kansas. Others devoted themselves to nonpolitical endeavors, often believing that African Americans should develop their own separate institutions rather than fight for existing ones to be opened to all races.

New court cases also eroded the rights of African Americans. In 1883, the Supreme Court nullified the Civil Rights Act of 1875, a law passed to affirm the equality of all persons in the use of transportation, hotels, inns, theaters, and other public places. Federal law no longer superseded state segregation measures.

Around the same time, several states passed railroad segregation laws. First, in 1881, Tennessee passed its law to segregate the railroads. Next, between 1887 and 1889, Florida, Mississippi, and Texas followed suit. The era of "separate but equal" facilities had begun.

Some African Americans accepted "separate but equal" as long as the accommodations were, in fact, equal. Booker T. Washington, for instance, said, "It is not the separation that we complain of, but the unequality of accommodations." The leading supporter of vocational education for blacks, Washington wondered why blacks could ride in the same streetcars as whites but not in the same trains. He traveled widely and complained about the inferiority of the Jim Crow car:

> The seats in the coach given to colored people are always greatly inferior to those given the whites. The car is usually very filthy. There is no carpet as in the first class coach. White men are permitted in the car for colored people. Whenever a poorly dressed, slovenly white man boards the train he is shown into the colored half coach. When a white man get drunk or wants to lounge around in an indecent position he finds his way to the colored department.

Such young activists as Louis Martinet and Homer Plessy, on the other hand, objected to the very notion of separation, even if the facilities were equal. They had grown up with new freedoms that had been denied their parents. They didn't want to see them slip away. In 1887, Homer Plessy became the vice president of the Justice, Protective, Educational and Social Club, a fifty-member organization dedicated to educational reform. In 1889, Martinet founded the *Crusader*, which billed itself as "newsy, spicy, progressive, liberal, stalwart and fearless."

The *Crusader* chronicled the increasing violence against African Americans, including an item about a mob attack that killed seven and wounded six laborers. "Are we in slavery times?" the *Crusader* asked. Indeed, Martinet couldn't help but wonder if the new laws his generation had helped to craft were about to become obsolete. When the Louisiana Separate Car case came before the Louisiana legislature in 1890, he was ready for a fight.

In 1925, New Orleans streetcars were segregated even though blacks, whites, and Creoles often lived together peacefully on the same street.

THree
POINT OF DEPARTURE:
THE SEPARATE CAR ACT

ON MAY 14, 1890, the Separate Car Act began its winding, unpredictable journey through the Louisiana state legislature.

The new bill innocuously called itself "an act to promote the comfort of passengers in railway trains." However, opponents saw the "comfort" as one-sided, intended for whites at the expense of blacks. The Separate Car Act required railroad officials to divide passengers by race. The first section of the statute read:

> That all railway companies carrying passengers in their coaches in this State, shall provide equal but separate accommodations for the white, and colored races, by providing two or more passenger coaches for each passenger train, or by dividing the passenger coaches by a partition so as to secure separate accommodations.

Louisiana defined "colored" as persons "belonging wholly or partly to the African race." Opponents of the bill bristled at its exemption for "nurses attending children of the other race." No exemption, however, existed for interracial families or friends traveling together, leading critics to believe that the bill's real intent was to put African Americans in a subordinate position despite its promise of "equal but separate." Representative Victor Rochon, for instance, found it insulting that whites would be willing to travel with "a dozen or perhaps more negro servants" but not with African Americans such as himself and his family. Newspaper publisher Louis Martinet and other community activists in a civil rights group called the American Citizens' Equal Rights Association declared, "Such legislation is unconstitutional, un-American, unjust, dangerous, and against sound public policy."

During debate on the bill, legislators aired their prejudice against immigrants as well as African Americans. Chinese and Italian immigrants, in particular, were singled out. The House of Representatives approved the Separate Car Act, then sent it to the Senate for consideration. At first, on July 8, 1890, the Senate voted against it. In an editorial the following day, the *New Orleans Times* criticized the Senate vote:

A man that would be horrified at the idea of his wife or daughter seated by the side of a burly negro in the parlor of a hotel or at a restaurant cannot see her occupying a crowded seat in a car next to a negro without the same feeling of disgust. The Louisiana Senate ought to step in and prevent this indignity to the white women of Louisiana, as the legislatures of other states have done.

Meanwhile, another piece of legislation aroused debate about the future of the state's lottery system. While Governor Francis T. Nicholls railed against the lottery as a form of gambling, supporters of the bill argued that the lottery contributed much-needed funds to the state. Ultimately, the bill passed. Bitter about the vote, antilottery legislators decided to punish blacks who had voted in favor of the lottery by bringing back the Separate Car Act for a new vote. This time, on July 10, 1890, the Separate Car Act won final approval.

A CONSTITUTIONAL BATTLE

Martinet quickly used the pages of the *Crusader* to call for action against the new law. Money poured in for a court challenge. From the start, Martinet and lawyer Albion Tourgée believed the Separate Car Act violated the Thirteenth and Fourteenth Amendments of the U.S. Constitution. First, they considered the Thirteenth Amendment, which outlawed slavery:

Amendment XIII (1865)
Section 1: Neither slavery nor involuntary servitude, except as a punishment for crime whereof the party shall have been duly convicted, shall exist within the United States, or any place subject to their jurisdiction.
Section 2. Congress shall have power to enforce this article by appropriate legislation.

Martinet and Tourgée believed that the Thirteenth Amendment banned not only slavery but also "badges of servitude," such as segregation. However, the text of the Thirteenth Amendment itself left such an interpretation open to question. Next, they turned to the more complex Fourteenth Amendment:

Amendment XIV (1868)
Section 1. All persons born or naturalized in the United States, and subject to the jurisdiction thereof, are citizens of the United States and of the State wherein they reside. No State shall make or

enforce any law which shall abridge the privileges or immunities of citizens of the United States; nor shall any State deprive any person of life, liberty, or property, without due process of law; nor deny to any person within its jurisdiction the equal protection of the laws.

By guaranteeing African Americans citizenship, the Fourteenth Amendment overturned Chief Justice Roger B. Taney's infamous decision in the *Dred Scott* case. Traditionally states, rather than the federal government, had granted rights to citizens. The Fourteenth Amendment gave this power to the federal government.

But what exactly did the phrase "equal protection under the law" mean for African Americans? While Martinet and Tourgée interpreted it as barring segregation, others believed it forbade only exclusion. The Fourteenth Amendment, some said, allowed railroads to separate passengers by race as long as they didn't exclude anyone.

The language of the Fourteenth Amendment, however, makes no mention of racial classification. The omission was no coincidence. During debate on the measure, Congress rejected language that would have struck down segregation. Instead of prohibiting states from making "any distinction in civil rights" based on "race, color, or descent," Congress substituted the more ambiguous phrase of "equal protection of the laws." Thus the Fourteenth Amendment steered clear of the issue of segregation.

At the time, the amendment's Republican sponsors assured Democratic opponents that the measure would not threaten state laws against interracial marriage because such laws treated blacks and whites as the same. The key factor, they argued, was that the penalties be the same for both races. Senator Jack M. Howard of Michigan

NEARLY ONE HUNDRED AFRICAN AMERICANS DIED IN THE 1873 COLFAX MASSACRE. ALMOST HALF WERE KILLED BY THE WHITE LEAGUE AFTER THEY SURRENDERED. MANY WHITE SOUTHERNERS FOUGHT VIOLENTLY AGAINST RACIAL EQUALITY.

THE FOURTEENTH AMENDMENT, PASSED AFTER THE CIVIL WAR, ALLOWED
AFRICAN AMERICANS TO VOTE AND TO SERVE ON JURIES. DURING THE NEXT
TWENTY YEARS, STATES PASSED LAWS THAT STRIPPED AWAY THOSE RIGHTS FOR
MANY YEARS.

offered an example to show that equality would mean
simply the absence of unequal penalties. "It prohibits the
hanging of a black man for a crime for which the white man
is not to be hanged," he said.

TENTH AMENDMENT—POLICE POWERS

Supporters of the Separate Car Act also believed they had
the Constitution on their side. In particular, they pointed
to the broad, undefined powers given to the state under
the Tenth Amendment. Referred to as the states' police
powers, this Amendment states:

Amendment X (1791)
The powers not delegated to the United States by
the Constitution, nor prohibited by it to the
states, are reserved to the states respectively, or to
the people.

The Tenth Amendment seemed particularly relevant,
considering the violence of the times. The escalation of
racial violence and lynching made segregation appear to
many people to be a reasonable use of the states' police
powers. Seen in this light, some historians view segregation as one of many reform-oriented strategies of the
Progressive Era to improve public life.

Lower court precedents

When Tourgée set out to research precedents for his case,
he found few cases to support his opposition to segregation—and many against it. Lower courts across the nation
had upheld "separate but equal" in cases involving school
segregation and transportation. With regard to education,
a Massachusetts court in 1849 ruled that a school could
deny five-year-old Sarah Roberts admission because she
was African American. In *Roberts* v. *City of Boston*, Chief
Justice Lemuel Shaw declared that segregated schools did
not violate the Massachusetts constitution's guarantee of
equality before the law.

Yet while public regulations generally supported
school segregation, they varied more widely with regard to
transportation. In New Orleans, for instance, whites and
blacks rode side by side on the crowded streetcars, which
had been successfully desegregated.

On the other hand, railroads had long directed African
Americans to the smoking car. Courts allowed railroads to
make their own rules and regulations as long as they were
"reasonable." The courts, for instance, found it reasonable

for railroads to establish ladies' cars even though they excluded unaccompanied men. But, to be reasonable, accommodations also needed to be equal.

"repugnancies" between the races

If trains could segregate by gender, could they then segregate by race? Courts generally answered yes, pointing to "repulsions" or "repugnancies" between the races. In the precedent-setting case of *West Chester and Philadelphia Railroad Company* v. *Miles*, of 1868, the Pennsylvania Supreme Court decided that the railroad had acted properly in ejecting Vera Miles, a black woman who refused to sit in the rear of the coach. In his opinion, Justice Daniel Agnew examined the question of whether or not race was a reasonable criterion for the classification of passengers. Was there such a difference between the races that they needed to be separated? Yes, he answered, describing feelings of aversion between the races:

> The danger to the peace engendered by the feelings of aversion between individuals of the different races cannot be denied. It is a fact with which the company must deal. If a negro takes his seat beside a white man or his wife or daughter the law cannot repress the anger or conquer the aversion which some will feel. However unwise it may be to indulge the feeling, human infirmity is not always proof against it. It is much wiser to avert the consequences of this repulsion of race by separation than to punish afterwards the breach of the peace it may have caused.

u.s. supreme court precedents

In the decades following passage of the Thirteenth and Fourteenth Amendments, the U.S. Supreme Court also heard a variety of cases involving state versus federal powers. These cases involved matters as varied as state regulation of butchers, federal response to white supremacists, segregation on a Louisiana steamboat, the selection of blacks on juries, the constitutionality of the 1875 Civil Rights Act, and the constitutionality of a separate-but-equal train law in Mississippi. Most decisions proved unfavorable to Homer Plessy.

Taken together, these six cases offered the Citizens' Committee a snapshot of how the Supreme Court might receive its argument on behalf of Plessy. As the precedents came together in chronological order, they showed how the Supreme Court's "strict constructionist" interpretations of the Thirteenth and Fourteenth Amendments chipped away at the civil rights gains of Reconstruction.

First, in 1873, the Supreme Court addressed the Thirteenth and Fourteenth Amendments in the *Slaughterhouse Cases*. At first glance, a case involving white butchers fighting a state monopoly in Louisiana might appear to have little to do with the Civil War amendments. However, the lawyer for the butchers argued that the Thirteenth and Fourteenth Amendments had been fundamentally designed to shift power from the state to the federal government. The Supreme Court, however, disagreed. In a 5 to 4 verdict, the Court narrowed the definition of "involuntary servitude" in the Thirteenth Amendment and denied that the Fourteenth Amendment took away the states' power of citizenship.

Next, in *U.S.* v. *Cruikshank* (1876), the Supreme Court examined the question of whether or not blacks attacked by white supremacists in Colfax, Louisiana, had been deprived of their citizenship rights under the Fourteenth Amendment. The Court decided that they had not because the Fourteenth Amendment applied only to the action of states and not of individuals. Once again, the Court had

anti-Chinese sentiment

When Louisiana's Separate Car Act came up for debate, anti-Chinese as well as anti-black sentiments flared.

Representative W. C. Harris, for instance, said he found Chinese and Italian immigrants "not as desirable citizens as the colored people." Throughout the nineteenth century, many white Americans derided the Chinese immigrants who came to the country during the Gold Rush as "heathens" and "pigtails."

In 1854, the California Supreme Court ruled in the case *The People* v. *Hall* that the Chinese belonged in the same category as blacks and American Indians. The court determined that the testimony of a Chinese man who witnessed a murder committed by a white man was not admissible because the Chinese belonged to "a race of people whom nature has marked as inferior, and who are incapable of progress or intellectual development beyond a certain point."

In the South, some plantation owners paid West Coast brokers one hundred dollars per head to replace black labor with Chinese. In the West, Chinese workers played a major role in building the transcontinental railroad. Because of the shortage of females on the American frontier and the competition from white workers, many of the new Chinese immigrant men took up "women's work," cooking, cleaning, and often opening up their own laundries.

The Chinese brought vices as well as virtues to their new neighborhoods. Chinatowns became famous for gambling halls, brothels, and opium dens. American authorities drafted legislation to ban such activities and decried the immorality of the Chinese. Lurid stories in the press denounced Chinese laundries as fronts for immoral

Labor groups, meanwhile, attacked the Chinese for being "coolies" rather than free workers. The term came from the Hindi word *qūli*, which derives from one of the Hindu castes. Because the new immigrants had to repay loans to the Chinese merchants who had paid for their journey to America, they worked for whatever wages they could.

While American employers found Chinese workers conscientious and dependable, labor groups considered them a source of unfair competition. Employers repeatedly used Chinese workers as strikebreakers, fueling the resentments of white workers. In 1882, around the time the United States erected the Statue of Liberty, Congress passed the Chinese Exclusion Act to restrict immigration from Asia.

Even after passage of the Chinese Exclusion Act, attacks against the Chinese persisted. In 1880, a mob in Denver destroyed most of the buildings in Chinatown and dragged a laundryman through the streets, kicking and beating him to death. Five years later, whites in Rock Springs, Wyoming, opened fire on Chinese immigrants competing with them for jobs in the mines. The Rock Springs Massacre of 1885 left twenty-eight Chinese dead and fifteen wounded. After sending federal troops to break up the disturbance, President Grover Cleveland concluded that the "experiment of blending the social habits and mutual race idiosyncrasies of the Chinese laboring classes with those of the great body of the people of the United States . . . proved by the experience of twenty years . . . in every sense unwise, impolitic, and injurious to both nations."

The Chinese challenged much of the restrictive legislation in court. In 1886, the case of *Yick Wo* v. *Hopkins* came before the U.S. Supreme Court. Yick Wo had been charged with violating a San Francisco ordinance requiring laundries in wooden buildings to get a permit from the board of supervisors. Since wooden buildings posed more of a fire hazard than brick or stone buildings, the law seemed like a reasonable exercise of the state's police power. However, the board of supervisors had granted permission to all but one of the non-Chinese applicants but none to the two hundred Chinese applicants. The Supreme Court ruled that, while the ordinance did not specifically discriminate against the Chinese, it was administered in a discriminatory fashion, in violation of the Fourteenth Amendment. The judge who wrote the majority decision in *Plessy* v. *Ferguson* would later argue that the Separate Car Act was a more reasonable law than San Francisco's laundry ordinance.

Segregation and Chinese exclusion remained the laws of the land until the middle of the twentieth century. In 1943, Congress repealed the Chinese Exclusion Act and, by the late 1940s, Chinese had gained citizenship rights. Chinatowns, once condemned as squalid, became popular public attractions. Still, the records of the nineteenth-century Chinese immigrants have preserved their struggle for equality.

offered a narrow interpretation of the Fourteenth Amendment.

Then, in 1878, the Supreme Court heard a case involving a black woman named Josephine DeCuir, who had sued after being ejected from a first-class cabin on a Louisiana steamship. DeCuir's lawyer contended that a law passed by the Louisiana legislature in 1869 prohibited common carriers from "discrimination on account of race or color." Even though DeCuir was traveling within the state, the U.S. Supreme Court ruled in *Hall* v. *DeCuir* that Louisiana's law had wrongly tried to regulate interstate commerce and so was unconstitutional.

In 1880, the Supreme Court issued one of its few decisions interpreting the Fourteenth Amendment in favor of black civil rights. In the case of *Strauder* v. *West Virginia* (1880), the Court held that the state of West Virginia's exclusion of blacks from juries violated the U.S. Constitution.

U.S. CIVIL RIGHTS Law overturned

Then, in 1883, the Supreme Court struck its biggest blow to equal rights. In the *Civil Rights Cases*, the Supreme Court ruled that most of the provisions of the 1875 Civil Rights Act were unconstitutional. The case grew out of five challenges to the Civil Rights Act's requirement that all people "be entitled to the full and equal enjoyment of the accommodations, advantages, facilities, and privileges of inns, public conveyances on land or water, theatres, and other places of public amusement."

In his decision, Justice Joseph P. Bradley declared that the federal government should not try to regulate the behavior of private parties. In addition, he argued that African Americans had emerged from slavery and should no longer be "the special favorite of the law."

Finally, in the case of *Louisville, New Orleans & Texas*

Railway Company v. *Mississippi* (1890), the Supreme Court upheld an 1888 Mississippi law requiring segregated railroad cars. However, while upholding the law, the Court left open the question of whether or not passengers could be required to sit in a particular car. This question would later come up in the landmark case *Plessy* v. *Ferguson*.

CHALLENGING "SEPARATE BUT EQUAL"

Tourgée and Martinet were determined to challenge the Separate Car Act on constitutional grounds. They believed that segregation was discriminatory even if the accommodations were, in fact, equal, which was rarely the case. "The gist of our case," Tourgée argued, "is the unconstitutionality of the assortment: *not* the question of equal accommodation. . . . the State has no right to compel us to ride in a car 'set apart' for a particular race whether it is as good as another or not."

The wording of the Separate Car Act, however, made it an elusive target. Was "equal protection of the law" incompatible with separation by race? Louisiana's law skirted the issue by treating blacks and whites alike. Tourgée maintained that the wording of the law disguised its real purpose. "Its real purpose is to keep negroes out of one car for the gratification of whites—not to keep whites out of another car for the comfort and satisfaction of the colored passenger," he wrote.

Gauging from past experience, Tourgée would have an uphill climb making his case. Still, he was ready to begin the climb. The courtroom drama was about to begin.

four
DESTINATION:
THE LOWER COURTS

HOMER PLESSY'S TRAIN RIDE brought him exactly where he wanted to go. With his successful arrest, members of the Citizens' Committee set their test case in motion. Plessy was released on five hundred dollars' bail on June 7, 1892, to await his court date.

On October 11, 1892, Plessy received notice that he would be arraigned, or called to court, two days later. Originally, the case was scheduled for a date months earlier, but the judge had delayed it for matters he considered more important. Assistant District Attorney Lionel Adams had filed charges against Plessy for violating the Separate Car Act. The bespectacled Adams was a seasoned prosecutor with a background as a criminal attorney.

Judge John Howard Ferguson headed up Section A of the district criminal court in New Orleans. His docket bulged with cases involving crimes such as aggravated assault, larceny, and embezzlement. The violation of a train ordinance seemed minor by comparison. Although Judge Ferguson had ruled against the Separate Car Act in the earlier case involving an out-of-state route, no one knew how the Massachusetts-born Ferguson would respond to a case involving segregation on an intrastate route. He had no clear position on racial issues.

JUDGE JOHN HOWARD FERGUSON

Judge John Howard Ferguson came to New Orleans as a young man in search of opportunities. He quickly found them. A carpetbagger from Massachusetts, he rose from lawyer to politician to judge. Ferguson brought with him his distinctly Puritan sensibilities. He was born in 1838 on the island of Martha's Vineyard, the son of a shipmaster. The temperance movement, which regarded alcoholic drink as morally destructive, found many supporters on the windswept island, including the young Ferguson.

In New Orleans, Ferguson soon found himself in a culture totally unlike Puritan Massachusetts. Pervasive gambling, drinking, and prostitution made New Orleans famous as the wayward sister of the South. Ferguson set up shop as a civil lawyer and married Virginia Earhart, the daughter of a liberal lawyer, who had declared, "Man is man, be the shade of his skin white, green, or black."

Unlike his Republican father-in-law, though, Ferguson found a niche for himself with the Louisiana Democrats. He won a seat on Louisiana's new legislature, created in 1877 at the end of Radical Reconstruction. His opportunity came at the expense of a black representative, Aristide Dejoie, who was expelled by the new lawmakers. As a lawmaker, Ferguson focused on efficiency, procedure, and constituent needs rather than any ideological or racial agenda.

During the 1892 elections, Ferguson campaigned for Democrat Murphy J. Foster, an antigambling candidate who won the election for governor. On June 30, 1892, Governor Foster tapped Ferguson for a judgeship vacancy. Ferguson was sworn in as the Section A criminal judge in

New Orleans on July 5, 1892, less than a month after Homer Plessy's train ride.

As a new judge, Ferguson took it upon himself to rid New Orleans of gambling. He made it clear that the police could no longer look the other way. They needed to enforce the law, which made gambling illegal. Before long, he would also voice support for the Separate Car Act.

In the years following his decision, legal segregation became a part of everyday American life, extending from sports teams to water fountains. Judge Ferguson died in 1915 after falling down on the street and suffering a cerebral hemorrhage. His obituary in the *New Orleans Times-Picayune* praised him as one who "took part in the struggle for white supremacy."

On October 13, 1892, Homer Plessy appeared before Judge Ferguson, the man whose name would be forever linked in history with his.

Local attorney James Walker handled Plessy's defense in the Louisiana courts.

In a letter to lead lawyer Albion Tourgée, newspaper editor Louis Martinet described Walker as a "good, upright, and conscientious man." Homer Plessy sat next to Walker at the defense table.

Walker argued that the case should be dismissed on constitutional grounds. He stated that his client was "orderly, well-dressed, and not intoxicated" at the time of his arrest. If he had been drunk or disorderly, that, rather than his racial identity, would have been reason to deny him a seat on the first-class train. In their brief, Tourgée and Walker maintained that the Separate Car Act gave the train conductor too much power in labeling passengers. They declared:

> Race is a legal and scientific question of great difficulty, and the state has no power to authorize any person to determine the same without testimony, or to make the rights and privileges of any citizen of the United States dependent on the fact of race. The state has no right to distinguish between citizens, any reason, privilege or immunity they may possess.

Walker filed a motion to delay the proceedings so the court could consider the constitutionality of the Separate Car Act. Judge Ferguson agreed to the delay. The next hearing would be later that month.

BACK IN COURT

On October 28, 1892, Plessy's lawyer and Louisiana's assistant district attorney met again in Judge Ferguson's courtroom. Once again, Walker argued that his client had purchased a first-class ticket and that the problem was not Plessy's behavior but, rather, the Separate Car Act itself. Plessy declined to give his race.

Assistant District Attorney Adams, in turn, defended the Separate Car Act as the proper use of the state's police powers. Adams contended that hostilities between the races made separating them reasonable. He argued that white passengers had a right to be separated from the "foul odors" given off by blacks.

After listening to the two arguments, Ferguson adjourned the court. In the coming days, Democrat Grover Cleveland won the presidential election, and New Orleans grappled with a general strike. Although proponents of the Separate Car Act argued that the two races had a natural aversion to each other, the interracial cooperation that took place during the general strike showed that they could sometimes unite behind a common cause.

On November 18, 1892, Judge Ferguson issued his decision. He maintained that the state had the power to regulate railroads that operated completely within its borders. His ruling supported state-mandated racial separation:

> There is no pretense that he was not provided with equal accommodations with the white passengers. He was simply deprived of the liberty of doing as he pleased, and of violating a penal statute with immunity.

At this point, the trial could have continued, with Plessy facing a twenty-five-dollar fine or a twenty-day jail sentence if found guilty. Instead, Plessy's lawyers petitioned the Louisiana Supreme Court to stop the trial from proceeding. The state supreme court agreed to hear the case, which would now be called *Ex parte Plessy*. (*Ex parte* is

Latin for "for one party," meaning the case was brought at the request of Plessy's lawyers).

LOCAL REACTION

Both sides reacted strongly to Judge Ferguson's decision. The conservative press in New Orleans predictably supported the ruling. The *Times-Democrat* declared:

> It is hoped that what [Judge Ferguson] says will have some effect on the silly negroes who are trying to fight the law. The sooner they drop their so-called "crusade" against "the Jim Crow Car" and stop wasting their money in combating so well-established on principle—the right to separate the races in cars and elsewhere—the better for them.

Speaking against the decision, the *Crusader* criticized the *Times-Democrat* for using the term "silly negroes." Writer and Citizens' Committee member Rodolphe Desdunes spoke proudly of his race's contributions to Louisiana. He maintained:

> These "silly Negroes" . . . feel keenly the oppression which is saddled upon them for purposes of gain and power by individuals who have no better claim than brute force at their command. These "silly Negroes" and their ancestors have built up this country from its incipiency and have defended its soil at the cost of their blood and treasures.

TO THE LOUISIANA SUPREME COURT

In their brief to the Louisiana Supreme Court, Tourgée and Walker argued that the Separate Car Act violated both the Thirteenth and Fourteenth Amendments. In their view, the Thirteenth Amendment prohibited not only

Begging Letters

Historians call them "begging letters."

Men and women facing financial ruin in the late nineteenth century wrote letters to such wealthy industrialists as John D. Rockefeller and Andrew Carnegie, pleading for help. Although tales of rags to riches had captured the public imagination, true-life stories of the down-and-out were far more numerous. Begging letters reflected the Victorian sentimentality of the time.

One of those letters came from Emma Tourgée, the wife of Homer Plessy's lawyer, Albion Tourgée. Emma's letter to oil tycoon John D. Rockefeller Sr. was typical of the thousands he received each week in the 1890s. The letters generally began with an apology for intruding, then described the writer's financial troubles, and ended by describing the relief requested.

"You doubtless know who my husband is," Emma Tourgée began in her letter of September 26, 1890. She justified her writing to Rockefeller as an act of "a wife's devotion to her husband." Emma went on to describe her husband as an idealist who had "done some good to humanity in the past" and, with Rockefeller's help, could do more in the future. "He is no businessman," she explained. Instead, he was "a proud, sensitive man, battling with ill-health and ill-fortune." To lift the family out of debt, Emma asked for a no-interest loan of $25,000, offering her husband's $30,000 life insurance policy as collateral. In closing, she wrote, "Whether my plea is heard or not, I feel I have done no wrong, and what a true, loving woman will do for her husband—that is not wrong!"

Letters like Emma Tourgée's prompted the devout and detail-oriented Rockefeller to establish his own charitable foundation. Reviewing his many letters, he found a pattern—four-fifths were seeking funds for personal use

He preferred to help the other fifth, who were looking to assist others.

Not surprisingly, Rockefeller declined Emma Tourgée's request. The Tourgées struggled for the next several years. Emma bought groceries on credit and sold fruit from their orchard for extra cash. In an 1893 diary entry, she confessed her lack of confidence in her husband: "I have no faith in what he is doing—merely wasting time which should be given to other work, whereby we could have something to live on," she wrote. Albion Tourgée, in turn, struggled with his guilt for failing to provide for his family. His life continued on a downward spiral. One contemporary observer described Tourgée's appearance before the Supreme Court on behalf of Homer Plessy in 1896 as "another fool's errand," referring to his autobiographical novel *A Fool's Errand*, about a carpetbagger fighting for racial justice. In 1898, Tourgée published another autobiographical novel, *The Man Who Outlived Himself*. In this tale about a debt-ridden man, he wrote, "There is no crime the world will not forgive sooner than failure."

slavery but also the stigma of racial inferiority it perpetu-
ated. But, while the Thirteenth Amendment was important
to them, they anchored their case on the Fourteenth
Amendment. They believed the Separate Car Act violated
three provisions of the Fourteenth Amendment: 1.) the
privileges and immunities of United States citizens, 2.) due
process of the law, and 3.) equal protection.

Amendment XIV (1868)
Section 1. All persons born or naturalized in the
United States, and subject to the jurisdiction
thereof, are citizens of the United States and of the
State wherein they reside. No State shall make or
enforce any law which shall abridge the privileges
or immunities of citizens of the United States; nor
shall any State deprive any person of life, liberty,
or property, without due process of law; nor deny
to any person within its jurisdiction the equal protection of the laws.

First, with regard to "privileges and immunities" of
citizenship, they believed that, since the former slaves had
acquired full citizenship, states could not legitimately
make distinctions between the races when it came to
accommodations.

Next, the idea of due process deals with fairness,
requiring guarantees such as clearly written laws applied
equally to all. Tourgée and Walker argued that the law con-
tained inexact phrases such as "persons of the colored race."
Such language, they believed, made the law overly vague.
Moreover, as a result of such ambiguous language, Homer
Plessy and others, for whom "the African admixture" was
"not perceptible," might be assigned to either a white or
colored coach, depending on the conductor's whim.

Third, the Separate Car Act violated the equal protection

requirement. For instance, the exemption for nurses showed that the real intention of the law was to ensure the comfort of whites at the expense of blacks. Furthermore, by exempting the railway and its officers from civil liabilities, Louisiana deprived a person of the right to sue for damages if wrongly expelled from the train.

arGumenTs For THe STaTe oF Louisiana

Assistant District Attorney Adams conceded that this provision exempting railways from civil liability should be withdrawn. By conceding this point, lawyers for the state of Louisiana undercut much of Plessy's due process argument. Passengers who felt they had been wrongfully assigned to a coach could sue for damages.

But what about someone who felt that assignment by race, in itself, violated the Thirteenth and Fourteenth Amendments? Speaking for the state of Louisiana, Attorney General Milton J. Cunningham and his associates pointed to a long list of legal precedents in their favor. First, they argued that the U.S. Supreme Court had upheld the constitutionality of a Mississippi law similar to the Separate Car Act. In the case of *Louisville, New Orleans & Texas Railway Company* v. *Mississippi* (1890), the Supreme Court had upheld Mississippi's right to segregate trains within its state limits, although it left open the question of whether or not passengers could be required to sit in a particular coach.

Next, Louisiana's lawyers showed that the U.S. Supreme Court already had agreed on a strict interpretation of the Thirteenth Amendment. In the *Civil Rights Cases*, the Court had rejected the notion that separation by race constituted a "badge of slavery."

Finally, they maintained the primacy of states' rights in matters pertaining to segregation as a reasonable use of the Tenth Amendment police powers. "The regulation of the civil rights of individuals is unquestionably a proper subject for the exercise of a State's police power, and laws passed to such regulations have been universally held constitutional and valid, except in extreme cases," maintained Attorney General Cunningham, Assistant District Attorney Adams, and attorney Alexander Porter Morse in their brief. They argued that segregation laws were a reasonable use of the state's police power as long as the regulations were equitable. Because the Separate Car Act provided for substantially equal accommodations (a previous court ruling had determined that "equality of accommodation did not mean *identity* of accommodation") and applied to whites as well as blacks, they argued, it was a "reasonable regulation."

Louisiana Supreme Court Decision

On December 19, 1892, Justice Charles E. Fenner rendered his decision for the Louisiana Supreme Court. First, he maintained that prior Supreme Court decisions had ruled out any application of the Thirteenth Amendment to the Separate Car Act.

Next, he turned to the Fourteenth Amendment. Justice Fenner pointed to two lower-court decisions in the North decided before ratification of the Fourteenth Amendment to show that segregation was not discriminatory. The first case came from the 1849 Massachusetts court decision allowing school segregation. In his decision in *Roberts v. Boston*, Chief Justice Lemuel Shaw had argued that segregation did not cause prejudice since "this prejudice, if it exists, is not created by law and [probably] cannot be changed by law."

The second case involved the Pennsylvania Supreme Court's decision in *West Chester and Philadelphia Railroad Company* v. *Miles* from 1867, allowing the railroad to require separate, racially divided cars. Justice Daniel

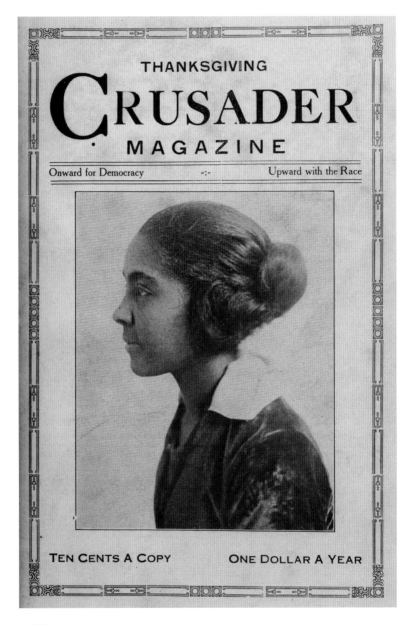

MARTINET, WHO REFUSED TO BE INTIMIDATED, PUBLISHED ARTICLES IN THE *CRUSADER* URGING AFRICAN AMERICANS TO FIGHT FOR THEIR RIGHTS. FOR A TIME, IT WAS THE ONLY AFRICAN-AMERICAN DAILY IN THE UNITED STATES.

Agnew justified segregation on the basis of cultural tradition and religious teaching. He argued that God had created the races dissimilar so that they did not "overstep the natural boundaries He has assigned to them." Although both decisions predated the passage of the Fourteenth Amendment, Fenner pointed out that they had occurred in states in which the civil rights of African Americans were fully recognized. He also pointed to the decisions made in most courts throughout the nation, which upheld segregation. He echoed Justice Agnew's view of the natural antipathy between the races. He maintained that to force "the company of one race upon the other . . . would foster and intensify repulsion between them rather than to extinguish it." Agreeing with District Attorney Adams that the Separate Car Act was a legitimate exercise of state power, Fenner noted that the law was not discriminatory, since it applied equally to both races. Addressing the opposition of African Americans to the Separate Car Act, he wondered why they would want to ride in cars where they were not wanted:

> Even were it true that the statute is prompted by a prejudice on the part of one race to be thrown in such contact with the other; one would suppose that to be sufficient reason why the pride and self-respect of the other race would equally prompt it to avoid such contact if it could be done without the sacrifice of equal accommodations.

NEXT STOP: U.S. supreme court
By ruling against Homer Plessy, the Louisiana Supreme Court opened the door for another appeal, this time to the nation's top court. Plessy's lawyers had wanted their case to go this high-profile route all along. Meanwhile, the *Times-Democrat* lauded Fenner's decision.

The two races will not mix, any more than oil and water, and it is better that the fact should be recognized at once, and made binding on both races by a law which will render all deliberate attempts at mixing penal [punishable].

On January 5, 1893, Tourgée and Walker filed for a hearing before the U.S. Supreme Court. The year ahead would be pivotal. Before long, the case that had moved so swiftly through the Louisiana courts would be derailed.

FIVE
CASE DERAILED

WHEN 1893 BEGAN, the case of *Plessy* v. *Ferguson* appeared to be chugging along, making its way toward the Supreme Court. Within a few months, though, its progress stalled. Activist Louis Martinet and lawyer Albion Tourgée surveyed the troubled times and didn't like what they saw. Racial tensions had intensified with the Panic of 1893 and the resulting depression. Across the South, lynchings occurred with startling frequency. Hundreds of black men unjustly accused of raping white women or of committing minor crimes such as loitering were captured by white mobs, taken to the woods, beaten, and then killed. Thousands of spectators watched and cheered, giving the lynchings a carnival-like atmosphere.

Martinet wondered if he was making a mistake by urging African Americans to fight for their rights when doing so might put their lives at risk. Other black leaders encouraged African Americans to keep to themselves, leave the South, or emigrate to Africa. Even some activist black leaders who seemed like natural allies doubted the wisdom of pursuing the *Plessy* v. *Ferguson* court challenge.

Much to Martinet's disappointment, the famous abolitionist Frederick Douglass refused to get involved in the fight against the Separate Car Act. Douglass, who had spoken out against lynching, explained that a court loss would set a bad precedent. In a letter to Tourgée, Martinet described how the fiery Douglass had reprimanded the Citizens' Committee for addressing its letter to Hon Fred Douglass instead of to his proper name, which was Frederick Douglass.

> His name was Frederick Douglass, he said, and he expressed his disapproval of the project & refused to give any aid. He saw no good in the undertaking—no good in protesting against encroachments on your rights? Was that a dodge to protect his pocket? Of course we were not after his money—we wanted his endorsement and moral support.

In 1893, Martinet spent part of the year as a medical student in Chicago. Being in Chicago helped him see the problems of the South in a new light. Other blacks from Louisiana had moved to Chicago permanently, and Martinet understood why. Life seemed easier in the North. Martinet wondered how best to improve the lives of blacks living in the South. In his May 30, 1893, letter to Tourgée, he asked, "The question forces itself upon me, are we fighting a hopeless battle—a battle made doubly hopeless by the tyranny and cruelty of the Southern white?"

When Martinet returned to Louisiana, he found conditions were worse than when he had left. Paul Bonseigneur, the Citizens' Committee member who had posted bond for Homer Plessy, had been forced to abandon his home in Covington, Louisiana, after threats from hostile white neighbors. Martinet spoke out against the repression. "Let Us Meet and Protest," declared the flyers for the crowded meeting he led. To further the cause of racial equality, Martinet published a pamphlet that summer titled *The Violation of a Constitutional Right*.

FREDERICK DOUGLASS, A FORMER SLAVE, WAS ONE OF THE COUNTRY'S MOST WELL KNOWN AFRICAN-AMERICAN ABOLITIONISTS. DOUGLASS DECLINED TO HELP FIGHT THE *PLESSY* CASE BECAUSE HE THOUGHT AN UNSUCCESSFUL VERDICT—WHICH HE CORRECTLY ANTICIPATED—WOULD HURT THE CAUSE OF RACIAL EQUALITY.

Tourgée Proposes a Delay

Tourgée, meanwhile, pondered the possible outcomes of *Plessy* v. *Ferguson*. As summer gave way to fall in his home in Mayville, New York, he weighed the chances of victory in the nation's Supreme Court. A new court appointment might shift the opinion of the body even farther away from the support of black civil rights. In a somber letter to Martinet dated October 31, 1893, Tourgée wrote:

> Of the whole number of Justices there is but one who is known to favor the view we must stand upon. One is inclined to be with us legally but his

political bias is strong the other way. There are two who may be brought over by the argument. There are five who are against us. Of these one may be reached, I think, if he "hears from the country" soon enough.

As a result, he suggested a new, two-part strategy: refrain from trying to advance the case, and mobilize public sentiment against Jim Crow. Tourgée asked Martinet to present his suggestions to the Citizens' Committee and encouraged him to continue the fight for equality. Meanwhile, Tourgée kept up his own organization, the National Citizens' Rights Association, which he had founded in 1891 to further the cause of racial equality.

Martinet's Citizens' Committee agreed with Tourgée's plan. To further mobilize public opinion, the *Crusader* went from weekly to daily publication in 1894. The expansion, though, came at a time of financial struggle. The printers and laborers agreed to work for half pay. The editors worked for free. Moreover, Martinet turned down a $1,200 annual stipend to study in Europe because he felt that his place was in New Orleans.

The new *Daily Crusader* proclaimed itself a friend of honest politics, education, labor, and justice. It also boasted of being the only Republican daily south of the Mason-Dixon line. Like its weekly predecessor, the *Daily Crusader* (published in both French and English) protested segregation and legislative attempts to ban interracial marriage. In 1894, the Louisiana legislature prohibited interracial marriage and amended the Separate Car Act to segregate railroad waiting rooms as well as cars. That same year, Congress ended funding for federal marshals and supervisors of elections, thus giving the South more leeway for disenfranchising blacks. If anything, the forces behind segregation were gaining, rather than losing, steam.

Scientific Racism

Science must be right.

That, anyway, was the way many people in the nineteenth century thought. Because science was supposedly objective, a steady stream of new studies gave greater validity to old theories of white supremacy.

In the 1830s, the new "science" of craniometry, the study of the physical dimensions of the human skull and brain, rose to prominence. Samuel George Morton (1799–1851), a Philadelphia physician and anatomy professor, pioneered the field. Working with skulls sent to him from naturalists and army surgeons around the world, Morton measured brain capacity by filling his specimens with white pepper seed, then emptying and measuring the contents. In 1839, he reported his finding that skulls differed by race, descending in cranial capacity from Caucasian to Ethiopian. The greater the cranial capacity, he concluded, the more advanced the race. According to Morton, the Caucasian possessed "the highest intellectual endowment" while the Ethiopian was "joyous, flexible, and indolent." The American media and Southern writers, too, described blacks as mentally inferior, childlike, and lazy.

Charles Darwin's theory of evolution, presented in *On the Origin of Species* (1859) and *Descent of Man* (1871), added a new justification for racial hierarchies. Darwin, an Englishman, believed that humans could be ranked on a hierarchy from savage to civilized, with the "lower races" filling the gap between animals and civilized people.

Darwin's cousin Francis Galton brought evolution squarely into the social domain. Galton coined the phrase "nature versus nurture," coming down strongly on the side of nature. In *Hereditary Genius*, published in 1869, he argued that mental ability was genetically determined. As one of the leaders of the eugenics movement, Galton believed that governments should take steps to encourage breeding among the best people and keep them from mixing with their inferiors. He argued that blacks were at least two grades below white Anglo-Saxons in ability and intelligence.

Sociologist Herbert Spencer, in turn, developed the field of social Darwinism in the 1860s and 1870s. Spencer described the evolutionary struggle as "the survival of the fittest," a phrase he, not Darwin, coined. In his racial hierarchy, whites stood above the lower races—American Indian, Polynesian, and African—whose lack of self-restraint and self-discipline kept them in a permanently childlike, or savage, state. Spencer's idea provided a rationale for subordinating African Americans and restricting the flow of immigrants into the United States.

By the mid-1890s, numerous prominent authorities argued that differences between the races were fixed and biologically determined, making the establishment of racial equality a false hope. Common medical opinion, too, held that blacks had deteriorated mentally, morally, and physically as freedmen and women. Popular depictions showed blacks as only one step removed from apes. In 1890, Edward Cope, a respected paleontologist at the University of Pennsylvania, warned:

> The highest race of man cannot afford to lose or even to compromise the advantages it has acquired in hundreds of centuries of toil and hardship for by mingling its blood with the lowest . . . The greatest danger which flows from the presence of the negro in this country is the certainty of the contamination of the [white] race.

While the lawyers in *Plessy* v. *Ferguson* were getting ready to present their case, statistician Frederick Hoffman was finishing up his manuscript for the book *Race Traits and Tendencies of the American Negro*. He wrote to his editors at the American Economic Association that his statistical research shed better light on the question of race than the "many foolish utterances" made by optimists such as Homer Plessy's lawyer Albion Tourgée. Hoffman's paradigm of scientific racism remained the norm until the 1911 publication of *The Mind of Primitive Man* by anthropologist Franz Boas. Revolutionizing the field of anthropology, Boas separated biology from culture, rejecting the notion of a racial hierarchy.

BOOKER T. WASHINGTON: "SEPARATE AS THE FINGERS"

On September 18, 1895, Booker T. Washington delivered a speech that caught the ear of the nation. In his famous Atlanta Compromise speech at the Atlanta Cotton States and International Exposition, Washington advanced the idea that African Americans should put aside their struggle for social and political equality until they had lifted themselves up economically. He used the metaphor "separate as the fingers" to describe his acceptance of segregation in social matters.

Washington's own life story illustrated his belief in the importance of hard work. Born a slave in Virginia in the spring of 1856, the young Booker went without shoes until the age of eight. He worked in his master's kitchen. Because it was illegal for slaves to be educated, the closest he got to school was carrying books for one of the master's daughters. "I had the feeling that to get into a schoolhouse

BOOKER T. WASHINGTON, SEEN HERE AT THE TUSKEGEE INSTITUTE IN ALABAMA, BELIEVED THAT AFRICAN AMERICANS SHOULD PROVE THEMSELVES EQUAL BY WORKING HARD RATHER THAN BY FIGHTING FOR THEIR RIGHTS IN THE COURTS.

and study would be about the same as getting into paradise," he later wrote.

After the Civil War, the ten-year-old Booker moved with his mother and stepfather to Malden, West Virginia, where he took a job at a salt mine. It began at 4 a.m., so he was able to attend school later in the day. Then, at the age of sixteen, he enrolled in Hampton Institute, a new school for blacks that allowed poor students to pay their way by working. The school emphasized the habits of thrift, industry, and practical know-how. Washington's years at the Hampton Institute shaped his basic beliefs and led him to create a similar school in Tuskegee, Alabama, in 1881.

Washington built the Tuskegee Institute literally from

Back-To-Africa Movement

Many blacks living in the racially charged terrain of the American South in the late nineteenth century dreamed of moving to greener pastures.

Some found those pastures on the American frontier following Benjamin "Pap" Singleton to Kansas, where he established a colony whose goal was to give blacks a better life. Others headed north, particularly to Chicago. But for many, the "homeland" of Africa held a special allure.

In the 1890s, letters poured into the American Colonization Society, an organization founded in 1817 to facilitate emigration to Africa. Many of the letters came from poor black tenant farmers who felt far removed from Booker T. Washington's middle-class life, which he achieved through accommodation. In a typical letter to the American Colonization Society, one man from Georgia wrote:

> We have little or no voice here & our wages are so small we scarcely have enough to subsist upon. . . . We feel like children away from home and are anxious to get home. We are quite sure that the U.S. of America is not the place for a colored man.

The movement back to Africa embodied two parallel often contradictory, trends: colonization and emigration. On the one hand, conservative white Americans proposed colonization as a way to get rid of blacks. On the other hand, black radicals embraced emigration as a solution to the problems their people faced fitting into American society.

In 1817, the American Colonization Society founded the settlement of Liberia in West Africa with funds from white philanthropists and support from the federal and state governments. The society maintained that its objective was

The controversial Back-to-Africa movement became popular in the 1890s, but former slaves had been settling in Liberia since 1817, funded by the American Colonization Society. Members of the Liberian Senate, many of whom were freed slaves from America, posed for this photograph in 1893.

to put free blacks where they could best use their talents. However, few free blacks volunteered to join the colony. Instead, most of the 13,000 African Americans transported to Liberia before the Civil War were ex-slaves whose masters had freed them on the condition that they leave the United States.

The Back-to-Africa movement was controversial from the start. In its early years, many blacks opposed it because they worried that the U.S. government would forcibly deport them to Africa. Interest in emigration waned during the Civil War and Reconstruction. Then, with the end of Reconstruction, Africa fever once again picked up steam.

During the years of violence, depression, segregation, and disenfranchisement, in the 1890s, new organizations and black leaders encouraged African emigration.

Leading the movement was Henry McNeal Turner (1834–1915), whose fascination with Africa dated back to his days of training for an African Methodist Episcopal (AME) church pastorate before the Civil War. Legend had it that Turner was the grandson of an African prince. As an AME bishop, Turner believed that Africa held redemption for his people. He encouraged his people to see their reflection in their deity, declaring, "We have every reason to believe that God is a Negro."

In 1894, four white men launched the International Migration Society to enter the emigration business not for charity but for profit. Turner and other prominent blacks served on the International Migration Society's advisory board. The society's plan called for would-be emigrants to pay a membership fee of one dollar, then one more dollar monthly, until they had accumulated forty dollars to pay for steamship passage and provisions.

Many poor blacks responded to the call, although considerably fewer managed to keep up the payments. Some scraped together what little they had, month after month, because of the glowing picture the International Migration Society painted of Africa. Joyous services marked by shouts of "Amen," "Hallelujah," and "God Bless Liberia" preceded one launching. Emigrants set off with high hopes. Expecting a land of gold and diamonds, hundreds of penniless emigrants found instead a nightmare of hunger and disease. Some survived the hard times and established prosperous farms. Others died or returned to the United States, bitter and disillusioned. Critics and disenchanted emigrants criticized the International Migration Society for swindling the destitute out of their life's savings. African-American leader Booker T. Washington faulted the migration movement for promoting escapism.

As criticism mounted and the economy worsened, the emigration movement faltered. The International Migration Society ceased its operations in 1899. Bishop Turner, who had been hailed as the "Black Moses," died in 1915. Soon after his death, a new leader, Marcus Garvey, revived the movement. Also called the Black Moses, the charismatic Garvey inspired a new sense of pride in the ancestral home in the 1920s. However, his leadership ended abruptly with his arrest for mail fraud and deportation to his native Jamaica. Since the 1920s, small emigration movements have come and gone, stymied by the difficulties of transporting large groups overseas. Still, the racial pride kindled by leaders such as Henry McNeal Turner and Marcus Garvey continues to burn on.

the ground up with a two-thousand-dollar grant from the Alabama legislature. Tuskegee focused on providing students with agricultural and industrial skills while instructing them to live modestly and work hard. Its message of economic self-help steered clear of the political messages that fueled white resentments in the South. By 1895, Tuskegee had grown into an impressive institution, and Washington had become a well-known figure in the national debate over race.

In his address at the opening ceremony of the prestigious Atlanta Cotton States and International Exposition on September 18, 1895, Washington argued that blacks needed to prove themselves worthy of the respect of whites. Rather than pose a threat by demanding immediate social and political equality, blacks should demonstrate their discipline through hard work and the mastery of a skilled trade. Washington believed that once blacks proved themselves capable of economic independence, social and political equality would follow. He called agitation for social equality "the extremist folly" and told his audience that

> No race can prosper till it learns that there is as much dignity in tilling a field as in writing a poem. It is at the bottom of life we must begin, and not at the top. Nor should we permit our grievances to overshadow our opportunities. . . . In all things that are purely social we can be as separate as the fingers, yet one as the hand in all things essential to mutual progress.

The audience responded with thunderous applause. Washington's speech offered a South plagued by violence and depression the promise of both racial calm and economic vitality. The *New York World* called Washington's speech "a revelation," "epoch-making," and a "turning point in the progress of the Negro race." President Grover Cleveland offered similar praise in a letter congratulating Washington on his speech. "I thank you with much enthusiasm for making the address," President Cleveland wrote. "Your words cannot fail to delight and encourage all who wish well for your race."

court date approaches

As newspapers across the nation hailed Washington's speech, Tourgée's and Martinet's calls for racial equality sounded increasingly out of tune with the times. The debate about gold-backed versus silver-backed currency seemed more pressing than the question of segregation. Populists joined forces with the Democratic Party, moving away from earlier messages of interracial cooperation. The faltering economy took a toll on both Martinet's and Tourgée's publications.

In July 1895, Martinet wrote to Tourgée that *Plessy v. Ferguson* had been docketed for the fall term. In his letter, Martinet thanked Tourgée for his "kindness and generosity" and encouraged him to feel better. Tourgée suffered from periodic bouts of depression. "It saddened me to receive your last letter," Martinet wrote. "You must get well & live. We need you yet. This is selfish—but then we love you too."

Lawyers on both sides of the case got to work on their briefs. Tourgée's dramatic prose comprised the bulk of the argument, with additional briefs provided by co-counsel James Walker and attorney Samuel Phillips. Attorney General Milton J. Cunningham represented the state of Louisiana by enclosing copies of the previous briefs and decisions rather than by furnishing new arguments.

Meanwhile, Frederick Douglass, an African-American leader who symbolized the fight for racial

STUDENTS AT THE TUSKEGEE INSTITUTE RECEIVED ACADEMIC AND VOCATIONAL TRAINING. IN ADDITION TO CHEMISTRY LABS, THE SCHOOL OFFERED COURSES IN PRACTICAL AREAS SUCH AS FARMING, BLACKSMITHING, AND CARPENTRY.

equality, had died, marking the end of an era. In December 1895, Tourgée gave a public eulogy for Douglass. Tourgée attributed Douglass's reluctance to get involved in the *Plessy* case to disillusionment with the way the Fourteenth Amendment was being interpreted. In his speech, Tourgée argued that Douglass's last wish was for a new generation of black activists to carry forward his life-long struggle for civil rights. "Let the life of Frederick Douglass be an example to those who must take up the conflict where he was obliged to lay it down," Tourgée declared. Although Tourgée's speech was applauded in the black press, the mood of the country had changed. Agitation for black rights had given way to talk of a new era of racial harmony based on Booker T. Washington's message of accommodation.

The Supreme Court was conservative at the time that *Plessy* v. *Ferguson* was heard. Standing (left to right): Justices George Shiras Jr., Rufus Wheeler Peckham, Stephen Johnson Field, and Horace Gray. Seated (left to right): Justices Henry Billings Brown and John Marshall Harlan, Chief Justice Melville W. Fuller, and Justices David Josiah Brewer and Edward Douglass White.

SIX
THE FINAL STOP:
SUPREME COURT

ALBION TOURGÉE BOARDED THE TRAIN from his
home in Mayville, New York, for the last leg of *Plessy* v.
Ferguson's legal journey. Oral arguments before the
Supreme Court in Washington, D.C., were scheduled for
Monday, April 13, 1896. Tourgée knew he'd be facing an
uphill battle. His delaying tactic had backfired. If anything, the country was more, rather than less, in favor of
segregation.

At the helm of the Supreme Court was the conservative
Chief Justice Melville W. Fuller. Justice Fuller initiated the
"conference handshake" to remind justices that while
their opinions might differ, they shared a common purpose. With his silver hair and thick, droopy mustache, he
bore a striking resemblance to the author Mark Twain.

Two new conservative-leaning justices had joined the
Court since 1892: Edward D. White, who had served in
the Confederate army, and Rufus W. Peckham, who championed business interests. One justice, David Josiah
Brewer, did not take part in the proceedings, offering no
reason for his absence. The maverick John Marshall Harlan
was the only justice on the bench who consistently supported African-American civil rights.

In 1896, the Supreme Court met in the old Senate

chamber of the U.S. Capitol. The accommodations were so tight, the justices had to change into their robes in full view of spectators. Scheduled argument sessions always began with the court marshal calling, "The honorable, the chief justice and the associate justices of the Supreme Court of the United States." As the justices entered the court, the marshal gave the traditional call for silence: "Oyez! Oyez! Oyez! All persons having business before the honorable, the Supreme Court of the United States, are admonished to draw near and give their attention, for the court is now sitting. God save the United States and this honorable court."

Unfortunately, the Court did not keep transcripts of its proceedings in the nineteenth century, so historians have had to piece together a picture of oral arguments from the lawyers' briefs and personal records. Lawyers for both sides had thirty minutes to make their arguments. Tourgée prepared notes for his argument, which historians have used to reconstruct the proceedings. Alexander Porter Morse represented the state of Louisiana.

PLESSY'S arguments

Albion Tourgée offered a wide-ranging defense of Homer Plessy, with some arguments tailored to appeal to the conservatism of the Court. "It is better to have too many points . . . than not enough," he remarked in a letter to his co-counsel, James Walker. Tourgée appealed to the Fuller Court's support of laissez-faire business interests by portraying whiteness as property under the Fourteenth Amendment. Arguing that membership in the dominant race was property "in the same sense that a right of action or inheritance is property," he asked, "how much would it be worth to a young man entering upon the practice of law, to be regarded as a white man rather than a colored one?"

Then Tourgée got to the heart of his constitutional argument. The intention of the Thirteenth Amendment,

Supreme Court Traditions

Traditions dating back centuries help give the Supreme Court its air of hallowed dignity. Soon after its creation, in 1790, the justices engaged in a heated debate about what to wear. They decided against English-style wigs brought over from France, where the monarch Henry II apparently wore one to conceal his premature baldness, and in favor of judicial robes, which could be traced back to the Roman toga. Black robes started being worn as mourning apparel after the death of Charles II, in 1685 but, because the gowns were more comfortable and less expensive than regular attire, they caught on for permanent use. The American judiciary adopted them even though Thomas Jefferson would have preferred that the justices wear plain suits.

At first, the Supreme Court justices wore black robes with a red facing. By 1800 they had switched to all black, perhaps to distance themselves from the British redcoats. Most, but not all, state supreme court justices also wear black robes. In Michigan, the supreme court justices wear red and, in Idaho, royal blue.

Some U.S. Supreme Court justices have added a couple of personal touches to the plain black robe. The late Chief Justice William Rehnquist added four gold stripes to each sleeve of his robe. Former Justice Sandra Day O'Connor, the first female justice, accented her robe with a long white collar when she joined the Court, in 1981. Justice Ruth Bader Ginsburg, who joined the Court in 1993, adopted similar neckwear. After Justice Rehnquist's departure, the new chief justice, John Roberts, kept wearing his plain black robe instead of making his predecessor's gold stripes the new tradition.

Chief Justice Melville Fuller, whose Court ruled on *Plessy v. Ferguson*, initiated the "conference handshake," a tradition that remains to this day. Each of the justices shakes hands with the other eight to symbolize that, while their opinions might differ, they share an overall harmony of purpose. In chambers, the chief justice still sits in the center. The most senior associate justice sits to the right of the chief justice, the justice with the next longest tenure to his left, and so on. Seniority also determines the order in which the justices vote and speak during conferences.

White quill pens, too, have become a signature element of the Court. They are placed on the counsel tables much as they were in the Court's earliest sessions.

Less bound by tradition, though, has been the location of the Supreme Court. Until 1935, the Court had no permanent building of its own, its meeting place changing more than a half dozen times. During the War of 1812, the British set fire to the Capitol, forcing the Court out of its quarters on the lower level. The Court held sessions in a local tavern described as "uncomfortable, and unfit for the purpose for which it was used."

William Howard Taft, the only U.S. president who also served as a Supreme Court justice, began pushing for better accommodations for the Court upon becoming chief justice in 1921. "In our conference room," Taft complained, "the shelves have to be so high that it takes an aeroplane to reach them." Chief Justice Taft won approval for the Supreme Court to have its own building but, unfortunately, he died five years before the stately new building opened its doors.

Another relatively new tradition is the longevity of Supreme Court justices. In the early years, the Court held less sway than it does now, prompting some justices to leave in favor of other pursuits. Prominent lawyers, such as Alexander Hamilton, declined invitations to join the bench. Now, the average tenure of a Supreme Court justice is about 26.1 years, up from an average of 14.9 years between 1789 and 1970. While new traditions have taken shape, the old ones have lingered. One of the most notable traditions of all is the Court's ability to keep its inner workings secret. Unlike other branches of the federal government, the Court remains virtually leak-proof. The loyal staff and tight security keep the Court out of the public glare. Once the justices put on their black robes, they follow many of the same procedures of their predecessors from hundreds of years ago. Court still begins with the Middle English call for "Hear Ye": "Oyez! Oyez! Oyez!"

he declared, was to abolish not only the institution of slavery but also "legal subjection and statutory inferiority to the dominant race."

The Fourteenth Amendment, he argued, had shifted the power to convey citizenship from the state to the federal government. "This provision of Section I for the Fourteenth Amendment *creates a new* citizenship of the United States embracing new rights, privileges and immunities, derivable in a *new* manner, controlled by new authority, having a *new* scope and extent, dependent on national authority for its existence and looking to national power for its preservation," Tourgée asserted. Even though the Supreme Court had interpreted the Fourteenth Amendment narrowly in rulings such as the *Slaughterhouse Cases* (1873) and *Cruikshank* (1876), he said, the decision in *Strauder* v. *West Virginia* (1880) showed the force of the country's new direction. The *Strauder* decision held that trying blacks by juries that excluded them was a violation of the Fourteenth Amendment.

In addition, Tourgée emphasized the ambiguities of race. How, he asked, could railroad officials categorize people by race when racial mixing was so prevalent that it was virtually impossible to categorize people? Although the Separate Car Act professed equal accommodations, Tourgée maintained that the Separate Car Act's exemption for nurses showed that its real intention was to keep African Americans subordinate.

In a memorable line from his brief, Tourgée reminded the justices of America's democratic tradition. "Justice is pictured blind and her daughter, the Law, ought at least to be color-blind," he declared. He stated that sorting passengers by race opened the door for the state to impose other forms of discrimination. To dramatize his point, he asked, "Why may it not require all red-headed people to ride in a separate car?"

Tourgée ended his argument by having justices imagine waking up with "a black skin and curly hair." How would they feel if they, too, were sent to the Jim Crow car? Predicting their response, he exclaimed, "What humiliation, what rage would then fill the judicial mind!"

Louisiana's Arguments

Attorney Alexander P. Morse, a Washington, D.C., lawyer who specialized in constitutional cases, spoke for the state of Louisiana. Going into the oral arguments, he had a long list of precedents on his side. In addition, the Louisiana Supreme Court's decision to hold the railroads liable for civil damages had undercut some of Plessy's due process and equal protection arguments. If passengers believed they had been wrongfully assigned to a coach, they could sue for damages.

Morse began his arguments by addressing the question of why the state segregated railroads but not streetcars (also known as "street railroads"). He contended that passengers on streetcars tended to be more accustomed to racial diversity than those on railroads, thus making segregation less of a necessity:

It is to be observed that "street railroads" are exempt from the operation of this statute. Sufficient reason for the exemption of this mode of transit appears from the fact, which will be noticed, that street railroads are only possible in thickly populated centres, where the white and colored races are numerically, in a ratio of equality, enjoy a more advanced civilization, and where the danger of friction from too intimate contact is much less than it is in the rural and sparsely settled districts.

Next, Morse argued that the Separate Car Act was "reasonable" because it applied "equally to white as to colored persons." He added that "equal accommodations" did not mean *identity* of accommodations.

Finally, Morse addressed the question of whether or not the Fourteenth Amendment gave the federal government control over the states. He argued that in matters involving social as opposed to political rights, authority fell primarily to the state under its police powers. Morse pointed to the decision in the *Civil Rights Cases* (1883) as an example of the right of states to exercise their police powers without restriction from the federal government.

Winding up his argument, he cited numerous precedents to show the Separate Car Act as one of many instances of racial segregation approved by the courts. He rejected an argument by Tourgée's co-counsel, Samuel Phillips, distinguishing between regulations for education and those for transportation. Instead, Morse held that cases involving school segregation also applied to transportation. He maintained that policies of racial separation have been used "from time immemorial":

> It is argued . . . that color is no ground for discipline or police. But color and race have been frequently the subject of police regulation in many of the States. And provisions in the laws and in the ordinances of municipalities have, from time immemorial, recognized and upheld the exercise of police power on the basis of color and race.

the majority decision

A little more than a month later, on May 18, 1896, Justice Henry Billings Brown delivered the 7 to 1 majority decision in *Plessy* v. *Ferguson*. Justice Brewer did not participate in the *Plessy* decision, so eight, rather than nine, judges decided the case. Justice Brown, who was considered a moderate to conservative judge, spoke for the majority, with Justice John Marshall Harlan dissenting.

Justice Brown's decision reflected the Court's reluctance to use the power of the federal government to protect the rights of private citizens. The judge began by stating the facts of the case, including that Homer Plessy was seven-eighths white and one-eighth black and had the appearance of a white man. Then Justice Brown addressed the question of whether or not the Thirteenth Amendment, which outlawed slavery, applied to the Separate Car Act. He maintained that it clearly did not. Explaining that the *Slaughterhouse Cases* and *Civil Rights Cases* had already defined slavery narrowly, he quoted from Justice Joseph P. Bradley's decision in the *Civil Rights Cases*:

> It would be running the slavery question into the ground to make it apply to every act of discrimination which a person may see fit to make as to the guests he will entertain, or as to the people he will take into his coach or cab or car, or admit to his concert or theater, or deal with in other matters of intercourse or business.

Next, Justice Brown considered the equal protection provisions of the Fourteenth Amendment. Making the common distinction between political and social rights, he argued that "in the nature of the things" the Fourteenth Amendment "could not have been intended to abolish distinctions based upon color, or to enforce social, as distinguished from political equality, or a commingling of the two races upon terms unsatisfactory to either." Justice Brown's use of the phrase "in the nature of things" indicated that he believed in a natural order that put whites at the top of a racial hierarchy.

Justice Brown described segregation as a common use of the state's police power. Laws calling for the separation of the races, he asserted, "have been generally, if not universally, recognized as within the competency of the state legislatures in the exercise of their police power." He pointed to laws allowing school segregation and prohibiting interracial marriage as accepted uses of the state's police power.

Turning to the *Civil Rights Cases* of 1883, he argued that the states—not the federal government—had jurisdiction over matters such as citizens' access to inns, theaters, and public transportation. Next, he mentioned a precedent closer to home: the *Louisville, New Orleans & Texas Railway Co.* v. *Mississippi* (1890) decision upholding the constitutionality of Mississippi's separate car law. The case sprang from Mississippi's suit against a railroad company for failing to provide separate cars as required by state law. The Court decided that the state law superseded interstate commerce regulations within its borders but left open the question of whether passengers could be forced to use the Jim Crow car. The case of *Plessy* v. *Ferguson* would provide the answer.

At issue for Justice Brown was the question of whether or not the Separate Car Act was "reasonable." If so, it would fall within the scope of the state's use of its police powers. As an example of an "unreasonable" regulation, Justice Brown pointed to the principle established in *Yick Wo* v. *Hopkins* (1886). The case of *Yick Wo* involved a San Francisco ordinance that licensed laundries in the name of the public good. Although the ordinance made no mention of ethnic or racial groups, the Supreme Court decided that it was administered in a way that discriminated against Chinese laundry owners and so violated the Fourteenth Amendment. Similarly, Justice Brown asserted that Tourgée's hypothetical law against redheads would also be found "unreasonable."

Justice Brown concluded that the Separate Car Act, on the other hand, was "reasonable" since it applied equally to both races:

In determining the question of reasonableness it [the state] is at liberty to act with reference to the established usages, customs and traditions of the people and a view to the promotion of their comfort, and the preservation of the good public peace and good order. Gauged by this standard, we cannot say that a law which authorizes or even requires the separation of the two races in public conveyances is unreasonable, or more obnoxious to the Fourteenth Amendment than the acts of Congress requiring separate schools for colored children in the District of Columbia, the constitutionality of which does not seem to have been questioned, or the corresponding acts of state legislatures.

Next, Justice Brown pointed to what he saw as two "fallacies," or illogical points, in Tourgée's arguments. First, he rejected Tourgée's argument that segregation laws put African Americans in a subordinate position. "If this be so," he argued, "it is not by reason of anything found in the act, but solely because the colored race chooses to put that construction upon it." Second, he disputed the notion that social prejudices could be overcome by legislation. "If the two races are to meet upon terms of social equality, it must be the result of natural affinities, a mutual appreciation of each other's merits and a voluntary consent of individuals," he argued.

In closing, Justice Brown addressed the question of "what constituted a colored person, as distinguished from a white person." He concluded that, since standards varied, state laws would provide the answer.

justice john marshall harlan's dissent

Justice John Marshall Harlan issued an eloquent dissent, providing the lone voice of opposition to the majority opinion. Known as the "Great Dissenter," Justice Harlan was the only consistent voice of support for African-American rights on the bench. Although a former slave-holder, he had come to insist on expansive interpretations of the Thirteenth and Fourteenth Amendments. His impassioned dissent in *Plessy* v. *Ferguson* repeated Tourgée's metaphor about "color-blind" justice.

Justice Harlan began his opinion by reiterating his belief that the railroads were public highways. He argued that the Separate Car Act's real intention was to gratify whites at the expense of blacks despite its guarantees of equal conditions. "Every one knows that the statute in question had its origin in the purpose not so much to exclude white persons from railroad cars occupied by blacks, as to exclude colored people from coaches occupied by or assigned to white persons," he declared. "'Personal liberty,' it has been well said, 'consists of the power of locomotion, of changing situation, or removing one's person to whatsoever places one's own inclination may direct . . .'"

Disagreeing with Justice Brown's argument about the authority states should have to implement "reasonable regulations," Justice Harlan emphasized the importance of adhering to the Constitution. He maintained that some people might find it "reasonable" to separate people by religion or to restrict one side of the street to whites and the other side to blacks.

In a rousing call echoing Tourgée's brief, he declared, "Our constitution is color-blind, and neither knows nor tolerates classes among citizens. In respect of civil rights, all citizens are equal before the law. The humblest is the

THe GreaT DISSenTer

Justice John Marshall Harlan went from being a slave-holder in Kentucky to the Supreme Court's leading advocate for black civil rights. "Let it be said that I am right rather than consistent," he explained.

The turbulence of the times helped explain some of his inconsistency. Born on June 1, 1833, in Boyle County, Kentucky, John Marshall Harlan grew up the son of lawyer and politician James Harlan, who named his son after the great Supreme Court justice, John Marshall. The Harlan family owned slaves but treated them with paternalistic goodwill. One day, father and son were on their way to church when they came across a brutish white man driving slaves to market. "You are a damned scoundrel," James Harlan said, shaking his forefinger with disapproval at the slave driver. The incident left a lasting impression on the young boy.

John Harlan followed in his father's footsteps, becoming a lawyer and politician. In his early twenties, he joined the anti-immigrant Know-Nothing Party. After marrying Malvina Shanklin, Harlan fought in the Civil War to keep Kentucky, a border state, in the Union. Finally, in 1868, he made his fateful switch to the Republican Party. Although he never spelled out the reason for his political conversion, the growth of white vigilante violence against blacks may have played a key role as he had witnessed his father's objections to the violent treatment of African Americans at an early age.

In April 1877, President Rutherford B. Hayes nominated Harlan to the Supreme Court. Despite criticism from Southern conservatives for Harlan's perceived weakness on states' rights and from Northern Republicans for s initial opposition to the Civil War Amendments, the Kentucky maverick won Senate confirmation on November 29, 1877. On December 11, 1877, he assumed his seat on the Supreme Court. He soon distinguished himself with his fiery oratory and ringing dissents.

In 1883, the *Civil Rights Cases* came before the bench. Justice Harlan's wife, Malvina, wrote about the difficulties her husband had writing his dissent. To provide inspiration, she retrieved the inkwell Justice Roger Taney had used to write the infamous *Dred Scott* decision. Malvina had squirreled away the old inkwell, knowing its historical importance. I have put a bit of inspiration on your study table," she told her husband. "I believe it is just what you need and I am sure it will help you."

Malvina Harlan was right. The inkwell reminded her husband of the shame in denying blacks the right of citizenship. In disagreeing with the majority decision in the *Civil Rights Cases*, he insisted that the Thirteenth Amendment was intended to outlaw not only human bondage but also "badges of slavery." In *Plessy* v. *Ferguson* he was the lone dissenter, the sole voice of opposition to "separate but equal."

Justice Harlan cared more about being true to his own beliefs than winning over his brethren. Although a less assured man might have adopted a more conciliatory stance out of fear of loneliness, Justice Harlan possessed an unflappable confidence in his own opinions. His dissents frequently showed impatience with his fellow justices' points of view.

Justice Harlan stayed on the bench until shortly before his death, on October 14, 1911. He often found himself at odds with his brethren, who exercised a laissez-faire approach to justice, deferring to business interests. "He could lead but he could not follow," said one speaker at his memorial service. "His was not the

mper of a negotiator." In the
es of subsequent conservative
stices, Justice Harlan's views
ere often regarded as the
oducts of an eccentric tem-
erament. Oliver Wendell
olmes referred to him as "the
st of the tobacco-spitting
dges" (at one time, tobacco
ewing was such an honored
adition on the Court that the
urt's furnishings included
ultiple spittoons).

In the 1950s, the civil
ghts movement rehabilitated
stice Harlan's reputation.
urgood Marshall, who served
the NAACP's lead lawyer in
e landmark case of *Brown
Board of Education*, found
spiration in Justice Harlan's

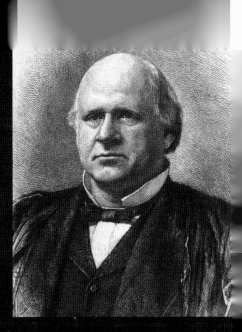

JUSTICE JOHN MARSHALL HARLAN WAS THE
ONLY DISSENTING JUSTICE IN THE *PLESSY* CASE.
DURING HIS THIRTY-FOUR YEARS ON THE
SUPREME COURT, HARLAN REMAINED A CONSIS-
TENT PROPONENT OF EQUAL RIGHTS FOR
AFRICAN AMERICANS.

essy v. *Ferguson* dissent. Marshall went on to become the
st black Supreme Court justice. A longtime associate of
arshall's, Constance Baker Motley, recalled,

Marshall's favorite quotation was, "Our Constitution is color-blind.". . . It became our basic
creed. Marshall admired the courage of Harlan
more than any Justice who has ever sat on the
Supreme Court. Even Chief Justice Earl Warren's
forthright and moving decision for the Court in
Brown did not affect Marshall in the same way.
Earl Warren was writing for a unanimous
Supreme Court. Harlan was a solitary and lonely

peer of the most powerful. The law regards man as man, and takes no account of his surroundings or of his color when his civil rights as guaranteed by the supreme law of the land are involved."

As Justice Harlan saw it, the Thirteenth and Fourteenth Amendments had erased the "race line" from America's system of government. He argued that the Thirteenth Amendment prohibited not only slavery but also "badges of slavery or servitude" and that the Fourteenth Amendment's guarantee of citizenship implicitly protected blacks against "legal discriminations, implying inferiority in society, lessening the security of their enjoyment of the rights which others enjoy, and discriminations which are steps toward reducing them to the condition of a subject race."

Yet, for all his egalitarian pronouncements, Justice Harlan was not free of prejudice. He shared the common anti-Chinese sentiments of his day. "There is a race so different from our own that we do not permit those belonging to it to become citizens of the United States," he began. "I allude to the Chinese race. But by the statute in question, a Chinaman can ride in the same passenger coach with white citizens of the United States, while citizens of the black race in Louisiana, many of whom, perhaps, risked their lives for the preservation of the Union . . . [are] declared to be criminals, liable to imprisonment, if they ride in a public coach occupied by citizens of the white race."

Still, Justice Harlan showed a prophetic understanding of the consequences the decision would have on the nation. He compared the majority's ruling to *Dred Scott* in exacerbating divisions within the nation. Warning that the majority decision in *Plessy* would perpetuate racial hatred, he declared:

The destinies of the two races, in this country, are indissolubly linked together, and the interests of both require that the common government of all shall not permit the seeds of race hate to be planted under the sanction of law. What can more certainly arouse race hate, what more certainly create and perpetuate a feeling of distrust between these races than state enactments, which, in fact, proceed on the ground that colored citizens are so inferior and degraded that they cannot be allowed to sit in public coaches occupied by white citizens? That, as all will admit, is the real meaning of such legislation as was enacted in Louisiana.

JIM CROW LAW.

UPHELD BY THE UNITED STATES SUPREME COURT.

Statute Within the Competency of the Louisiana Legislature and Railroads—Must Furnish Separate Cars for Whites and Blacks.

Washington, May 18.—The Supreme Court today in an opinion read by Justice Brown, sustained the constitutionality of the law in Louisiana requiring the railroads of that State to provide separate cars for white and colored passengers. There was no interstate commerce feature in the case for the railroad upon which the incident occurred giving rise to case—Plessey vs. Ferguson—East Louisiana railroad was and is operated wholly within the State, to the laws of Congress of many of the States. The opinion states that by the analogy of the laws of Congress, and of many of states requiring establishment of separate schools for children of two races and other similar laws, the statute in question was within competency of Louisiana Legislature, exercising the police power of the State. The judgment of the Supreme Court of State upholding law was therefore upheld.

Mr. Justice Harlan announced a very vigorous dissent saying that he saw nothing but mischief in all such laws. In his view of the case, no power in the land had right to regulate the enjoyment of civil rights upon the basis of race. It would be just as reasonable and proper, he said, for states to pass laws requiring separate cars to be furnished for Catholic and Protestants, or for descendants of those of Teutonic race and those of Latin race.

THE *PLESSY* V. *FERGUSON* VERDICT WAS NOT BIG NEWS IN THE MAINSTREAM PRESS, AS THIS SMALL CLIPPING FROM THE *NEW YORK TIMES* SHOWS. HOWEVER, ITS IMPACT WAS TO LAST FOR ALMOST A HUNDRED YEARS, WHEN THE SEPARATE-BUT-EQUAL DOCTRINE IT EMBRACED WAS OVERTURNED BY ANOTHER SUPREME COURT CASE: *BROWN* V. *BOARD OF EDUCATION*.

seven
MOVING ON: AFTERMATH
OF *PLESSY* V. *FERGUSON*

THE IMMEDIATE REACTION to the *Plessy* v. *Ferguson* verdict was relatively quiet, like the rumbling of a distant train. Unlike the reaction to the *Civil Rights Cases* thirteen years earlier, no mass protests greeted the decision. Newspaper coverage of *Plessy* v. *Ferguson* was sparse. The *New York Times* relegated its story to the section on railroad news rather than featuring it prominently on the front page. Other coverage ranged from the tacit endorsement of Southern whites to the outrage of the black press. Some white newspapers in the North, including the *Republican* of Springfield, Massachusetts, expressed surprise at and disapproval of the verdict. The *Republican* compared Jim Crow to the measles. "The law may be expected to spread like the measles in those commonwealths where white supremacy is thought to be in peril," the *Republican* predicted.

Soon after the decision, the Citizens' Committee disbanded, and the *Crusader* suspended publication. Of the $220 left in the Citizens' Committee budget, $160 went to charity and the remaining $60 to a testimonial for lead lawyer Albion Tourgée. Before disbanding, the Citizens' Committee issued one final statement, which contained the stirring phrase "we, as freemen, still believe that we were right":

Notwithstanding this [the Supreme Court's] decision . . . we, as freemen, still believe that we were
right and our cause is sacred. We are encouraged
by the indomitable will and noble defense of Hon.
Albion W. Tourgée, and supported by the coura-
geous dissenting opinion of Justice John Harlan
in behalf of justice and equal rights. In defending
the cause of liberty, we met with defeat, but not
with ignominy.

PLESSY RETURNS TO COURT

On January 11, 1897, Homer Plessy returned to Section A
of the criminal court to face the charge against him. The
Supreme Court's decision set the lower court's charge
back in motion. Plessy changed his plea from not guilty to
guilty. Offered a choice of paying a twenty-five-dollar fine
or spending twenty days in jail, Plessy chose the fine. By
his side were Citizens' Committee treasurer Paul
Bonseigneur and local attorney James Walker. After
paying the fine, Plessy returned to his place in the increasingly segregated world.

Segregation spread just as the Springfield, Massachusetts, newspaper predicted it would. It extended to virtually every aspect of life—from birth in segregated hospitals
to death in segregated cemeteries. New laws even extended
segregation to drinking fountains and public toilets. In
1902, a new state law prompted New Orleans to resegre-
gate its streetcars.

Homer Plessy returned to obscurity after the case.
With his days as a shoemaker cut short by the rise of factory-
made shoes, Plessy found work as a laborer, warehouse-
man, clerk and, finally, as a collection agent for a
black-owned insurance company.

Plessy's local attorney, James Walker, died in July
1898. Albion Tourgée died in 1905 in Bordeaux, France,

where he was serving as an American consul appointed by
President William McKinley. Judge John Ferguson died in
1915 at the age of seventy-seven. Louis Martinet died on
June 7, 1917, exactly twenty-five years to the day after
Homer Plessy's historic train ride. Plessy, the youngest of
the group, died in 1925. His obituary was as unassuming
as the man: "Plessy—on Sunday, March 1, 1925, at 5:10
a.m. beloved husband of Louise Bordenave."

As segregation became the law of the land, African
Americans found a variety of ways to cope. They came
together in churches and in their own organizations,
where they found strength and mutual support. Some
adopted Booker T. Washington's strategies of accommodation. Others left the American South to establish lives in
the North, in the West, or in Africa. Still others decided to
fight for equal rights.

Harvard-educated African American W. E. B. Du Bois
stood at the forefront of the new civil rights movement. In
1905, Du Bois called a meeting of nearly thirty African-
American leaders to draw up a list of demands for achieving
racial equality. Because habitable hotels in the United States
refused to accommodate blacks, the group met in Ontario,
Canada. They called themselves the Niagara Movement.
Echoing the sentiments of the Citizens' Committee, Du Bois
declared his opposition to Jim Crow: "We want discrimination in public accommodation to cease. Separation in
railway and street cars, based simply on race and color, is
un-American, undemocratic, and silly."

Although the Niagara Movement's powerful words
struck a chord with many African Americans, the group
failed to effectively translate their words into action. By
1910, the group had disbanded. The Niagara Movement,
however, laid the groundwork for the emergence of a bigger
and more powerful organization—the National Association
for the Advancement of Colored People (NAACP).

THE BIRTH OF THE NAACP

On February 12, 1909—the one-hundredth anniversary of the birth of Abraham Lincoln—white and black civil rights activists joined with the Niagara Movement to launch the National Association for the Advancement of Colored People (NAACP). In its first statement, the NAACP resurrected the ideals championed by Abraham Lincoln:

> If Mr. Lincoln could visit this country in the flesh, he would be disheartened and discouraged. . . . He would see the black men and women, for whose freedom a hundred thousand of soldiers gave their lives, set apart in trains, in which they pay first-class fares for third-class service, and segregated in railway stations and in places of entertainment; he would observe that state after state declines to do its elementary duty in preparing the Negro through education for the best exercise of citizenship.

Du Bois became the editor of the organization's publication, the *Crisis*, which he used as a powerful weapon to fight discrimination. He vividly chronicled incidents of racial violence and offered insightful commentaries on the political and educational struggles that African Americans faced. The *Crisis* also provided a forum for a new group of black writers and poets who, like Du Bois, had settled in Harlem, New York. In the 1920s, the Harlem Renaissance blended artistic expression with racial pride and activism.

In the 1930s and 1940s, U.S. presidents Franklin D. Roosevelt and Harry Truman issued executive orders to halt racial discrimination in the federal government and military. In addition, the NAACP mounted a steady stream of challenges to Jim Crow in court. At first, the NAACP focused on cases that showed clearly unequal accommodations. After winning a solid string of victories, the NAACP

WAR KNOWS NO COLOR LINE

MORE THAN TWO MILLION AFRICAN-AMERICAN MEN REGISTERED FOR THE
DRAFT DURING WORLD WAR II. THEIR HEROIC SERVICE—AND THE RACIAL
GENOCIDE HITLER PERPETRATED ON THE JEWS—SPURRED THE MOVEMENT
TOWARD INTEGRATION AND GREATER RIGHTS FOR AFRICAN AMERICANS.

embarked on the more ambitious goal of tackling the
"separate" part of "separate but equal."

World War II also helped generate support for racial
reform. Some Americans began to question policies of seg-
regation after seeing the tragic consequences of Adolf
Hitler's policies based on racial hatred. On June 5, 1950, the
Supreme Court ruled against segregation in the case of
McLaurin v. *Oklahoma State Regents*, maintaining that
African-American students must be treated like all other
students. The University of Oklahoma had relegated the

African-American student George McLaurin to a former broom closet next to a classroom and marked every place reserved for him with specially prepared signs reading "Colored."

Also in 1950, Supreme Court Justice Robert Jackson came across Albion Tourgée's brief for *Plessy* v. *Ferguson*. Writing to a friend, Justice Jackson noted Tourgée's use of the phrase "color-blind":

> He says, "Justice is pictured blind and her daughter, the Law, ought at least to be color-blind." Whether this was original with him, it has been gotten off a number of times since as original wit. Tourgée's brief was filed April 6, 1896, and now, just fifty-four years after, the question is again being argued whether his position will be adopted and what was a defeat for him in '96 be a post-mortem victory.

By the early 1950s, the NAACP had laid the groundwork for a case to fundamentally challenge Jim Crow. The legal team just needed to find the right plaintiff.

Before long, one appeared.

Brown v. Board of Education

Oliver Brown wanted his seven-year-old daughter, Linda, to go to an elementary school close to their house. Otherwise, she'd have to walk though a dangerous railroad yard. The nearby school, however, refused his request because the school was for whites only. An angry Oliver Brown brought the school's refusal to the attention of the NAACP, which helped him file suit against the Topeka, Kansas, school board. Years later, Linda Brown recalled,

> Both of my parents were extremely upset by the fact that I had to walk six blocks through a

dangerous train yard to the bus stop—only to wait,
sometimes up to half an hour in the rain or snow,
for the school bus that took me and the other black
children to "our school." Sometimes I was just so
cold that I cried all the way to the bus stop . . . and
two or three times I just couldn't stand it, so I came
back home.

The case of *Brown* v. *Board of Education* incorporated
five suits that were consolidated for hearing before the
U.S. Supreme Court. All challenged segregation in public
schools. At first, the Supreme Court seemed unsympa-
thetic to the petitioners. Then, on September 8, 1953,
Chief Justice Fred Vinson died suddenly of a heart attack,
and the case got a new start. The new chief justice was Earl
Warren, the former governor of California and an opponent of segregation.

Thurgood Marshall, the NAACP's lead lawyer, argued
the case for the petitioners. Marshall maintained that separate schools—even those with facilities equal to those in
white schools—were harmful to African Americans. To
make his case, he pointed to the research of African-
American psychologist Kenneth Clark, who was noted for
the "doll tests" he used to show the psychological harms of
segregation. When African-American children from segregated schools were shown one white and one black doll
and asked which doll was the "good" one, they usually chose
the white doll. Clark concluded that segregation harmed the
self-esteem of African-American schoolchildren.

Supporters of segregation, on the other hand, maintained that "separate but equal" policies served the public
good. Milton Korman, one of the lawyers for the defen-
dants, maintained that segregation held psychological
benefits for black children, who found "a receptive atmosphere" in their own separate schools.

Mendez v. Westminster

Before Linda Brown, there was Sylvia Mendez.

In 1947, the little-known case of *Mendez* v. *Westminster* ended the segregation of Mexican-American children in California public schools, thus paving the way for *Brown* v. *Board of Education*. *Mendez* v. *Westminster* never reached the U.S. Supreme Court because it was settled at the state level.

The case began after eight-year-old Sylvia Mendez was denied admission to the Seventeenth Street Elementary School. Like her older brothers, she went to the Hoover School, a two-room shack in the middle of Westminster's Mexican neighborhood. "I didn't understand why they wouldn't let my brothers and [me] in the nice school," Sylvia Mendez recalled. Her father, Gonzalo Mendez, organized the lawsuit, which involved four school districts, while her mother, Felicitas, tended to the family's agricultural business. Sylvia testified during the trial to show that Mexican-American students had the same capacity for learning as their white counterparts.

Two key players from *Brown* v. *Board of Education*—Thurgood Marshall and Earl Warren—were also involved in *Mendez* v. *Westminster*. Thurgood Marshall, the lead lawyer for the NAACP in the 1954 *Brown* case, filed a friend-of-the-court brief for Mendez on behalf of the NAACP. The *Mendez* case also influenced the thinking of California governor Earl Warren, who went on to become the chief justice of the Supreme Court at the time of *Brown* v. *Board of Education*. In June 1947, Governor Warren signed an order to officially outlaw segregation in California's public schools.

As a result of the lawsuit, Sylvia Mendez was allowed to attend the Seventeenth Street Elementary school. However, her experience was not an easy one, as she faced hostility from white students. "I would go home crying," she recalled. "'Why am I going to that school where I am not wanted?' My father simply told me, 'I fought for you to go there.'"

Mendez succeeded in school and became a nurse. She retired after thirty years in the field and began giving lectures about her family's story. Others, too, have awakened public interest in the case. In 2004, Mendez was invited to the White House for the celebration of National Hispanic Heritage Month. She met with President George W. Bush and shared her story with key Democrats, including U.S. Senator Hillary Rodham Clinton of New York. Then, on April 14, 2007, the U.S. Postal Service released a special commemorative stamp to mark the sixtieth anniversary of the *Mendez* v. *Westminster* ruling, shining a new spotlight on the long-neglected case.

"I want this case recognized as a historical presence," Mendez said during a presentation at the University of Central Florida. "I want it taught in history classes. We have come a long way, but we still have a long way to go."

Chief Justice Warren used the political skills he had gained as a long-term governor of California to unify a divided Court. He used male-bonding activities, such as baseball and fishing, to create a sense of camaraderie on the bench. After offering his own opinion against segregation, Chief Justice Warren encouraged the other members of the Court to come to their own consensus. The justices who originally supported segregation eventually came around to his point of view.

On Monday, May 17, 1954, Chief Justice Warren announced the Supreme Court's unanimous decision in

Brown v. *Board of Education.* "To separate [African-American children] from others of similar age and qualifications solely because of their race generates a feeling of inferiority as to their status in the community that may affect their hearts and minds in a way unlikely ever to be undone," he declared in his opinion. "We conclude . . . that in the field of public education the doctrine of 'separate but equal' has no place. Separate educational facilities are inherently unequal."

The *Brown* decision overturned more than half a century of Jim Crow law. Chief Justice Warren used the *Yick Wo* precedent to show that, even if a particular law seemed nondiscriminatory on the surface, it could be found to be discriminatory. The Supreme Court ruled in *Brown* that evidence not available in Plessy's time showed that legally mandated school segregation was not a "reasonable" use of the state's Tenth Amendment police powers.

Chief Justice Warren's decision avoided the question of whether racial classifications themselves violated the Fourteenth Amendment. Instead of adopting Justice Harlan's principle of a "color-blind" Constitution, he pointed to new evidence showing segregation to be unreasonable. "Whatever may have been the extent of psychological knowledge at the time of *Plessy* v. *Ferguson*," he declared, "this finding is amply supported by modern authority." He also emphasized the importance of public education to preserving a democratic society.

The chief justice knew that dismantling decades of segregation would be no simple matter. As a result, he scheduled a separate round of oral arguments and briefs for the implementation of desegregation, which came to be known as *Brown II*. In oral arguments for *Brown II*, the NAACP recommended that school desegregation begin immediately. States with segregated school districts, however, maintained that such a plan was impractical. The Court opted for a compromise of sorts, calling for desegregation to proceed with "all deliberate speed."

Meanwhile, buses had replaced trains as the standard means of urban transportation. On April 23, 1956, the Supreme Court ruled that segregated buses in Columbia, South Carolina, were illegal. Nevertheless, segregation persisted. In Montgomery, Alabama, Dr. Martin Luther King Jr., a twenty-six-year-old minister, led a bus boycott after African-American Rosa Parks refused to surrender her seat to a white passenger.

CIVIL RIGHTS Movement and Backlash

Throughout the South, white political leaders defied the new desegregation orders. King and a new generation of civil rights activists responded to segregation with peaceful protests. In 1963, the police in Birmingham, Alabama, greeted peaceful demonstrators with police dogs and fire hoses. Television coverage of the incident stirred the conscience of the nation. President John F. Kennedy reported that the images made him "sick."

Shortly after the assassination of President Kennedy, Congress passed the sweeping 1964 Civil Rights Act, championed by President Lyndon B. Johnson. Yet despite court decrees and new laws, old traditions of segregation lingered. In 1964, Supreme Court Justice Hugo Black said, of the progress toward desegregation since *Brown* v. *Board of Education*, "There has been entirely too much deliberation and not enough speed."

Conditions for blacks in the inner cities grew increasingly bleak, with unemployment rates double those for whites. In 1967, a series of riots broke out in black communities across the nation. The National Advisory Committee on Civil Disorders, appointed by President Johnson, concluded in its Kerner Report: "Our nation is moving toward two societies, one black, one white—separate and unequal." In the early 1970s, employers and universities launched new affirmative action programs to increase employment and educational opportunities for minorities.

Critics of the new affirmative action programs argued that no one should be able to get ahead on account of race. Citing the equal protection clause of the Fourteenth Amendment, some whites claimed to be the victims of reverse discrimination. In 1977, the case of *Regents of the University of California* v. *Bakke* came before the U.S. Supreme Court. The case involved Allan Bakke, a white male student denied entrance to the University of California Medical School at Davis. The *Bakke* case came before a deeply divided Supreme Court. Ironically, opponents of affirmative action claimed the mantle of Harlan's "color-blind" Constitution to argue that people should be judged on their own terms without regard to race. Supporters of affirmative action, including Thurgood Marshall (by that point a Supreme Court justice), on the other hand, maintained that race-conscious programs should be adopted to remedy prior discrimination. Justice Lewis Powell offered a compromise. While faulting the U.C. Davis admissions program as a "quota system," Justice Powell argued that schools could take steps to achieve a diverse student body.

African Americans, meanwhile, were divided in their responses to desegregation and affirmative action. Often, desegregation failed to live up to its promise. Many schools became unofficially resegregated as a result of "white flight." In racially mixed schools, whites and blacks often remained apart, separated by social mores and educational tracking. Some African-American leaders argued that black neighborhood schools might do a better job of instilling pride in students if their directors were not fighting for integration at any cost. As one school board member in Atlanta put it, "I don't believe it is necessary for a black child to sit next to a white child to get a good education."

In 1991, civil rights pioneer Thurgood Marshall retired from the Supreme Court. His seat went to the conservative Clarence Thomas, an African American opposed to affirmative action. In addition, a new generation of coalition-building African-American leaders, including Senator Barack Obama of Illinois, attracted multiracial support. For Obama, though, race still mattered. "We're going to have a lot of work to do to overcome the long legacy of Jim Crow and slavery," he said in 2007.

Thurgood Marshall

Thurgood Marshall got the nickname "Mr. Civil Rights" for good reason.

The first African-American justice on the Supreme Court, Marshall rocketed to fame as the lead attorney in *Brown* v. *Board of Education*. He was the grandson of slaves. Born on July 2, 1908, in Baltimore, Maryland, Marshall was the son of Norma Williams, a teacher, and William Canfield Marshall, a waiter at a whites-only country club. Marshall remembered his father telling him and his brother, "If anyone calls you a [racial epithet deleted], you not only got my permission to fight him, you got my orders to fight him."

In 1929, Marshall graduated with honors from Lincoln University, an all-black college near Philadelphia, but was denied admission to the University of Maryland Law School on the basis of race. Instead he attended Howard University Law School. After graduating (again with honors) from Howard University Law School in 1933, he went into private practice in Baltimore. In 1935, he won his first major civil rights victory, which ordered the University of Maryland Law School (where he had been denied admission) to admit its first African-American student.

Marshall continued chipping away at segregation as a lawyer for the NAACP. In 1940, he became director of the organization's newly formed Legal Defense and Educational Fund, a post he held until 1961. His ground-breaking victories struck down laws making it difficult or impossible for blacks to vote in primaries, serve on juries, or find housing. While arguing cases in the racially charged South, Marshall sometimes received death threats. In 1954, he accomplished his longtime goal of overturning *Plessy* v. *Ferguson*. "We struck the jackpot," Marshall later remarked about *Brown* v. *Board of Education*. In 1961, President John F. Kennedy chose Marshall for a federal judgeship. Four years later, Marshall became the nation's first African-American solicitor general. In 1967, President Lyndon B. Johnson nominated Marshall for an associate justice position on the U.S. Supreme Court. Marshall took his seat on October 2, 1967, becoming the nation's first African-American justice to sit on the U.S. Supreme Court.

During his near-quarter century on the Supreme Court, Marshall backed individuals' rights and measures to end discrimination, consistently voting with the liberal bloc. But, as presidents Ronald Reagan and George H. W. Bush took office in the 1980s, the Supreme Court became more conservative. The liberal voting bloc dwindled. Marshall joked that he was in the majority on only one issue: "breaking for lunch."

As his health declined, Justice Marshall expressed hope that President Bush would not replace him with "the wrong Negro." President Bush did, however, appoint conservative African-American Clarence Thomas to take his seat when Marshall resigned—Thomas's views are diametrically opposed to those of Marshall. Thurgood Marshall died in January 1993 at the age of eighty-four. He left a long legacy of contributions to civil rights, as attested to by the many schools named in his honor.

Controversies Linger

More than fifty years have passed since *Brown* v. *Board of Education* overturned *Plessy* v. *Ferguson*. In the summer of 2007, a deeply divided Supreme Court heard a case involving two school integration programs. The consolidated case of *Parents Involved in Community Schools* v. *Seattle School District* involved programs in Seattle, Washington, and metropolitan Louisville, Kentucky, that sought to maintain school diversity by limiting transfers on the basis of race or using race as a tiebreaker for admission to particular schools. In Seattle, where "white flight" had been common, the tiebreaking program was established to maintain racial balance. A nonprofit group, Parents Involved in Community Schools (Parents), argued that the racial tiebreaker policy violated the equal protection clause of the Fourteenth Amendment.

In a 5 to 4 vote, the Supreme Court agreed that such programs violated the Fourteenth Amendment, arguing that the goal of diversity did not justify the use of race in school selection. Chief Justice Roberts wrote in his opinion, "The way to stop discrimination on the basis of race is to stop discriminating on the basis of race."

Significantly, both the liberals and the conservatives on the bench claimed the mantle of *Brown* v. *Board of Education* in making their 2007 decision. On the one hand, the four conservatives—Chief Justice John G. Roberts Jr. and Justices Antonin Scalia, Clarence Thomas, and Samuel A. Alito Jr.—pointed to *Brown* as overturning policies based on race. On the other hand, the four liberals—Justices Stephen G. Breyer, John Paul Stevens, David H. Souter, and Ruth Bader Ginsburg—carried forth *Brown*'s spirit of racial tolerance. Liberal Justice John Paul Stevens criticized Chief Justice John G. Roberts's invocation of *Brown* as "a cruel irony."

Justice Anthony Kennedy, the man in the middle,

IN 2007, THE SUPREME COURT FOUND THAT THE USE OF RACE IN DETERMINING ADMISSION TO PUBLIC SCHOOLS WAS UNCONSTITUTIONAL. IRONICALLY, THIS CASE TURNED THE *BROWN* DECISION ON ITS HEAD TO ALLOW FOR SCHOOL SEGREGATION.

agreed with the conservatives that the two programs were unconstitutional but criticized Chief Justice Roberts's opinion for its "all-too unyielding insistence that race cannot be a factor in instances when, in my view it may be taken into account." In his separate opinion, Justice Kennedy described how the criterion of color blindness set forth in *Plessy* v. *Ferguson* differed from the strategies needed to achieve diversity in the twenty-first century.

The statement by Justice Harlan that "our Constitution is color-blind" was most certainly justified in the context of his dissent in *Plessy* v. *Ferguson*. The Court's decision in that case was a grievous error it took far too long to overrule. *Plessy*, of course, concerned official classification by race applicable to all persons who sought to use railway carriages. And, as an aspiration, Justice Harlan's axiom must command our assent. In the real world, it is regrettable to say, it cannot be a universal constitutional principle.

While much has changed since the *Plessy* v. *Ferguson* decision of 1896, one fundamental question remains the same. What constitutes the public good? In the nineteenth century, conservatives pointed to segregation. In the twenty-first century, liberals have argued that policies should take race into consideration in order to do away with lingering prejudice. Conservatives, on the other hand, want to do away with the consideration of race.

More than one hundred years ago, Albion Tourgée recognized that the term "color-blind" could have a negative as well as a positive meaning. In addition to keeping people from discriminating, color blindness could also mean nearsightedness. In his 1880 novel *Bricks without Straw*, Tourgée used the term to criticize the government for failing to see that the freedmen needed help improving their lives even though they had already gained legal rights. "The law was still color-blinded by the past," Tourgée wrote. More than a century later, Americans are still debating matters of color. Knowledge of the issues raised in *Plessy* v. *Ferguson* can help us navigate the best path for the future.

NOTES

Introduction

p. 8, par. 1, Anne Wallace Sharp, *A Dream Deferred: The Jim Crow Era* (Farmington Hills, MI: Lucent Books, 2005), 34.

p. 8, par. 2, Otto H. Olsen, ed., *The Thin Disguise: Plessy v. Ferguson.* (New York: Humanities Press, 1967), 117.

p. 8, par. 3, Olsen, *The Thin Disguise*, 119.

p. 8, par. 4, Sharp, *A Dream Deferred*, 96.

p. 8, par. 5, Erica Perez, "Children's Book on O.C. Desegregation Debuts," *Orange County Register* (12 September 2008), http://www.ocregister.com (accessed 13 July 2007).

Chapter 1

p. 11, par. 5, Harvey Fireside. *Separate and Unequal: Homer Plessy and the Supreme Court Decision that Legalized Racism* (New York: Carroll & Graf Publishers, 2004), 1.

p. 12, par. 4, Keith Weldon Medley. *We as Freemen: Plessy v. Ferguson* (Graetna, LA: Pelican Publishing, Co., 2003), 142.

Who Was Jim Crow?

p. 12, par. 1, Ronald L.F. David, Ph.D., "Creating Jim Crow: In-Depth Essay," http://www.jimcrowhistory.org/history/creating2.htm (accessed 23 July 2007).

p. 13, par. 2, Medley, *We as Freemen*, 142.

p. 13, par. 3, Medley, *We as Freemen*, 140.

p. 14, par. 2, Medley, *We as Freemen*, 16.

p. 19, par. 2, Medley, *We as Freemen*, 130.

p. 19, par. 4, Medley, *We as Freemen*, 153.

p. 20, par. 2, Charles A. Lofgren, *The Plessy Case: A Legal-Historical Interpretation* (New York: Oxford University Press, 1987), 32.

Albion Tourgée: A Life Like a Novel

p. 15, par. 3, Otto H. Olsen, *Carpetbagger's Crusade: The Life of Albion Winegar Tourgée* (Baltimore: The John Hopkins Press, 1965), 7.

p. 15, par. 3, Mark Elliott, *Color-Blind Justice: Albion Tourgée and the Quest for Racial Equality* (Oxford, UK: Oxford University Press, 2006), 54.

p. 16, par. 3, Olsen, *Carpetbagger's Crusade*, 67.

p. 16, par. 3, Edmund Wilson, *Patriotic Gore: Studies in the Literature of the American Civil War* (New York: W. W. Norton & Co., 1962), 532.

p. 16, par. 4, Elliott, *Color-Blind Justice*, 169.

p. 17, par. 1, Elliott, *Color-Blind Justice*, 167.

p. 17, par. 2, Keith Weldon Medley, *We as Freemen:* Plessy v. Ferguson (Graetna, LA: Pelican Publishing, Co., 2003), 61.

p. 17, par. 4, Elliott, *Color-Blind Justice*, 204.

p. 18, par. 1, Olsen, *Carpetbagger's Crusade*, 354.

p. 18, par. 2, Olsen, *Carpetbagger's Crusade*, 341.

p. 21, par. 1, Roger A. Fischer, *The Segregation Struggle in Louisiana: 1862–77* (Urbana: University of Illinois Press, 1974), 10.

p. 21, par. 2, Mark Golub, "Plessy as 'Passing': Judicial Responses to Ambiguously Raced Bodies in *Plessy v. Ferguson*," *Law & Society Review* (1 September 2005): 563.

p. 21, par. 2, Thomas J. Davis, "More Than Segregation, Racial Identity: The Neglected Question in *Plessy* v. *Ferguson*," *The Race and Ethnic Ancestry Digest* 10 (2004): 12.

p. 21, par. 4, Davis, "More Than Segregation," 12.

p. 21, par. 5, Medley, *We as Freemen*, 97.

p. 22, par. 1, Medley, *We as Freemen*, 104.

p. 22, par. 3, Lofgren, *The Plessy Case*, 29.

p. 23, par. 1, Lofgren, *The Plessy Case*, 30.

p. 24, par. 2, Mark Elliott, *Color-Blind Justice: Albion Tourgée and the Quest for Racial Equality* (Oxford, UK: Oxford University Press, 2006), 266.

Chapter 2

p. 25, par. 2, Norman Coombs, "Slavery as Capitalism," chapter three in *The Immigrant Heritage of America* (Twayne Press, 1972). http://www.rit.edu/~nrcgsh/bxcon.html (accessed 16 August 2007).

p. 25, par. 3, C. Vann Woodward, *The Strange Career of Jim Crow* (New York: Oxford University Press, 1974), 17.

p. 26, par. 1, Nathan Aaseng, *Plessy v. Ferguson* in *Famous Trials* (Farmington Hills, MI: Lucent Books, 2003), 17.

p. 27, par. 1, John. W. Blassingame, *Black New Orleans: 1860–1880* (Chicago: University of Chicago Press, 1973), 15.

Ladies' Cars

p. 29, par. 2, Barbara Young Welke, *Recasting American Liberty: Gender, Race, Law, and the Railroad Revolution, 1865–1920* (Cambridge, UK: Cambridge University Press, 2001), 289.

p. 30, par. 1, Welke, *Recasting American Liberty*, 284.

p. 30, par. 2, Pamela Newkirk, "Ida B. Wells-Barnett: Journalism as a Weapon Against Racial Bigotry," *Media Studies Journal* (Spring/Summer 2000): 26.

p. 30, par. 3, Amy G. Richter, *Home on the Rails: Women, The Railroad, and the Rise of Public Domesticity* (Chapel Hill: The University of North Carolina Press), 97.

p. 31, par. 1, Richter, *Home on the Rails*, 95.

p. 31, par. 3, Richter, *Home on the Rails*, 98.

p. 32, par. 1, "Japan Tries Women-Only Train Cars to Stop Groping," ABC News, (13 November 2006), http://abcnews.go.com/GMA/International/Story

p. 27, par. 3, Keith Weldon Medley, *We as Freemen: Plessy v. Ferguson* (Graetna, LA: Pelican Publishing, Co., 2003), 80.

p. 28, par. 2, Roger A. Fischer, *The Segregation Struggle in Louisiana: 1862–77* (Urbana: University of Illinois Press, 1974), 54.

p. 33, par. and p. 34, par. 1, Fischer, *The Segregation Struggle in Louisiana*, 58, 59

p. 34, par. 1, Fischer, *The Segregation Struggle in Louisiana*, 70.

p. 34, par. 2, Stephen G. Hall, "Revisiting the Tragic Era and the Nadir: Interrogating Individual and Collective African American lives in the Gilded Age and Progressive Era," *Journal of the Gilded Age and Progressive Era* (October 2005): 409.

p. 34, par. 5, Scott A. Sandage. *Born Losers: A History of Failure in America*. (Cambridge, MA: Harvard University Press, 2005), p. 228.

p. 35, par. 4, Hodding Carter, ed., *The Past as Prelude: New Orleans 1718–1968* (New Orleans: Tulane University, 1968), 296.

p. 36, par. 2, Carter, *The Past as Prelude*, 296.

p. 36, par. 3, Fischer, *The Segregation Struggle in Louisiana*, 134.

p. 38, par. 2, Woodward, *The Strange Career of Jim Crow*, 33.

p. 38, par. 3, Woodward, *The Strange Career of Jim Crow*, 49.

Tale of Terror

p. 37, par. 3–4, Brook Thomas, ed., *Plessy v. Ferguson: A Brief History with Documents* (Boston, MA: Bedford/St. Martin's, 1997), 1.

p. 37, par. 6, Thomas, *Plessy v. Ferguson*, 1.

p. 37, par. 8, Thomas, *Plessy v. Ferguson*, 3.

p. 38, par. 4, Medley, *We as Freemen*, 112.

p. 39, par. 2, Michael J. Klarman, "The Plessy Era," *Supreme Court Review* (Annual 1998): 303.

p. 39, par. 3, Michael J. Klarman, *From Jim Crow to Civil Rights: The Supreme Court and the Struggle for Racial Equality* (New York: Oxford University Press, 2004), 12.

p. 39, par. 3, Charles A. Lofgren, *The Plessy Case: A Legal-Historical Interpretation* (New York: Oxford University Press, 1987), 13.

p. 41, par. 1, Lofgren, *The Plessy Case*, 16.

p. 41, par. 2, Medley, *We as Freemen*, 104.

p. 41, par. 3, Medley, *We as Freemen*, 107.

Chapter 3

p. 43, par. 2, Keith Weldon Medley, *We as Freemen: Plessy v. Ferguson* (Graetna, LA: Pelican Publishing, Co., 2003), 96.

p. 43, par. 3, Charles A. Lofgren, *The Plessy Case: A Legal-Historical Interpretation* (New York: Oxford University Press, 1987), 29.

p. 43, par. 4, *Plessy* v. *Ferguson*, 163 U.S. 537 (1896). http://curiae.law.yale.edu

p. 43, par. 4, Brook Thomas, ed., *Plessy v. Ferguson: A Brief History with Documents* (Boston, MA: Bedford/St. Martin's, 1997), 52.

p. 44, par. 1, Medley, *We as Freemen*, 96–97.

p. 44, par. 3, Medley, *We as Freemen*, 100.

p. 45, par. 4–5, Thomas, *Plessy v. Ferguson*, 11–12.

p. 45, par. 6, Thomas, *Plessy v. Ferguson*, 14.

p. 46, par. 4, Mark Elliott, *Color-Blind Justice: Albion Tourgée and the Quest for Racial Equality* (Oxford, UK: Oxford University Press, 2006), 267.

p. 48, par. 1, Lofgren, *The Plessy Case*, 66.

p. 49, par. 1, U.S. Const., Bill of Rights. Cornell University Law School, http://www.law.cornell.edu/constitution/constitution.billofrights.html

p. 49, par. 2, Michael J. Klarman, "The Plessy Era," *Supreme Court Review* (Annual 1998): 303.

p. 50, par. 3, Lofgren, *The Plessy Case*, 119–120.

p. 55, par. 2, Harvey Fireside, *Separate and Unequal: Homer Plessy and the Supreme Court Decision that Legalized Racism* (New York: Carroll & Graf Publishers, 2004), 134.

Anti-Chinese Sentiment

p. 52, par. 2, Keith Weldon Medley, *We as Freemen:* Plessy *v.* Ferguson (Graetna, LA: Pelican Publishing, Co., 2003), 97.

p. 52, par. 2, Gretchen Dickey, "Downtown Opium Dens Attracted Many," (undated). http://www.epcc.edu/ nwlibrary/ borderlands/21_opium.htm

p. 52, par. 3, Center for Educational Telecommunications. "Ancestors in the Americas: *The People* vs. *Hall,*" (undated), http://lwww.cetel.org/1854_hall.htm (accessed 16 April 2007).

p. 52, par. 4, Roger Daniels, *Asian America: Chinese and Japanese in the United States since 1850.* (Seattle: University of Washington Press, 1988), 40.

p. 53, par. 1, Henry Kittredge Norton, "Gold Rush and Anti-Chinese Race Hatred" in *The Story of California From the Earliest Days to the Present*, 283–296, (Chicago: A. C. McClurg & Co., 1924), http://www.sfmuseum.org

p. 53, par. 3, Daniels, *Asian America*, 57.

p. 54, par. 1, U.S Department of State, "Basic Readings in U.S. Democracy, Part X, *Yick Wo* v. *Hopkins* (1886)," http:// usinfo.state.gov/usa/infousa/facts/democrac/64.htm (accessed 16 April 2007).

p. 55, par. 4, Lofgren, *The Plessy Case*, 71.

p. 55, par. 5, Thomas, Plessy *v.* Ferguson, 24.

p. 56, par. 2–3, Elliott, *Color-Blind Justice*, 263–264.

Chapter 4
Judge John Howard Ferguson

p. 58, par. 3, Keith Weldon Medley, *We as Freemen:* Plessy *v.* Ferguson (Graetna, LA: Pelican Publishing, Co., 2003), 45.

p. 59, par. 3, Medley, *We as Freemen*, 217–218.

p. 60, par. 3–5, Medley, *We as Freemen*, 161–162.

p. 61, par. 2, Peter Irons, "Jim Crow's Schools" in *Jim Crow's Children* (New York: Viking, 2002). http://www.aft.org/

pubsreposrt/american_educator/issues/summer04/crow
schools.htm (accessed 16 August 2007)

p. 61, par. 5, Medley, *We as Freemen*, 163.

Begging Letters

p. 63, par. 2, Scott A. Sandage, *Born Losers: A History of Failure in America*. (Cambridge, MA: Harvard University Press, 2005), 9.

p. 63, par. 4, Mark Elliott, *Color-Blind Justice: Albion Tourgée and the Quest for Racial Equality* (Oxford, UK: Oxford University Press, 2006), 272–273.

p. 63, par. 5, John D. Rockefeller, *Random Reminiscences of Men and Events* Project Gutenberg Consortia Center ebook, http:// www.gutenberg.org/etext/17090 (accessed 22 May 2007).

p. 64, par. 2, Elliott, *Color-Blind Justice*, 273.

p. 64, par. 3, Harvey Fireside, *Separate and Unequal: Homer Plessy and the Supreme Court Decision that Legalized Racism* (New York: Carroll & Graf Publishers, 2004), 193.

p. 64, par. 3, Sandage, *Born Losers*, 252.

p. 62, par. 3, Medley, *We as Freemen*, 166–167.

p. 62, par. 5, Medley, *We as Freemen*, 166–167.

p. 65, par. 2, Brook Thomas, ed., *Plessy v. Ferguson: A Brief History with Documents* (Boston, MA, 1997), p. 14.

p. 65, par. 4, Mark Elliott, "Race, Color Blindness, and the Democratic Public: Albion W. Tourgée's Radical Principles in *Plessy v. Ferguson*," *Journal of Southern History* (May 2001): 287.

p. 65, par. 4, Thomas J. Davis, "More Than Segregation, Racial Identity: The Neglected Question in *Plessy v. Ferguson*," *The Race and Ethnic Ancestry Digest* 10 (2004): 34.

p. 66, par. 4–p. 67, par. 1, *Plessy v. Ferguson*, 163 U.S. 537 (1896), http://curiae.law.yale.edu

p. 67, par. 3, Charles A. Lofgren, *The Plessy Case: A Legal-Historical Interpretation* (New York: Oxford University Press, 1987), 52.

p. 69, par. 1, Barbara Young Welke, *Recasting American Liberty: Gender, Race, Law, and the Railroad Revolution, 1865–1920* (Cambridge, UK: Cambridge University Press, 2001), 239.

p. 69, par. 2–3, Justice Charles E. Fenner, *Ex Parte Homer A. Plessy* in *Plessy* v. *Ferguson*, 163 U.S. 537 (1896) http://curiae.law.yale.edu

p. 70, par. 1, Medley, *We as Freemen*, 168.

Chapter 5

p. 71, par. 1, Louis Menand, "Morton, Agassiz, and the Origins of Scientific Racism in the United States," *The Journal of Blacks in Higher Education* (Winter 2001–2002): 110.

p. 72, par. 2, Dr. Jonathan Plucker, "Francis Galton," Indiana University. http://www.indiana.edu/~intell/galton. shtml (accessed 17 August 2007).

p. 72, par. 3, Constitutional Rights Foundation, "Social Darwinism and American Laissez-faire Capitalism," http://www.crf-usa.org/bia/bria19_2b.htm (accessed 17 August 2007).

p. 72, par. 4, Medley, *We as Freemen*, 179.

p. 73, par. 2–p. 74, par. 1, Medley, *We as Freemen*, 182.

p. 74, par. 3, Joseph LaQuinta, "The Crusader's Fight for Justice: A Look Back at a Daily Paper's Fight for Civil Rights," *New Orleans Unmasked* (2005), Xavier University. http://cat.xula.edu/unmasked/articles/435/ (accessed 1 July 2007).

p. 74, par. 4, Medley, *We as Freemen*, 186–187.

p. 77, par. 3, Booker T. Washington National Monument, "Biography," http://www.nps.gov/archive/bowa/btwbio.htm (accessed 12 June 2007).

Scientific Racism

p. 75, par. 3, John P. Jackson Jr., and Nadine M. Weidman, *Race, Racism, and Science: Social Impact and Interaction* (Santa Barbara, CA: ABC-CLIO, 2004), 47.

p. 75, par. 5, Jackson and Weidman, *Race, Racism, and Science*, 99.

p. 76, par. 2, Jackson and Weidman, *Race, Racism, and Science*, 78.

p. 76, par. 4, Charles A. Lofgren, *The Plessy Case: A Legal-Historical Interpretation* (New York: Oxford University Press, 1987), 108.

p. 77, par. 1, Brook Thomas, ed., *Plessy v. Ferguson: A Brief History with Documents* (Boston: Bedford Books, 1997), 99.

p. 78, par. 2 and p. 83, par. 1, "Booker T. Washington," *Contemporary Black Biography* 4. Biography Resource Center Online, Gale Research, 2007. http://galenet.galegroup.com/servlet/BioRC (accessed 1 July 2007).

p. 83, par. 3, Thomas, *Plessy v. Ferguson*, 122.

Back-to-Africa Movement

p. 79, par. 4, Edwin S. Redkey, *Black Exodus: Black Nationalist and Back-to-Africa Movements, 1890–1910* (New Haven, CT: Yale University Press, 1969), 8.

p. 79, par. 6–p. 80, par. 1, Redkey, *Black Exodus*, 18–19.

p. 81, par. 2, "Henry McNeal Turner," *This Far by Faith: African-American Spiritual Journeys*, PBS, June 24–26, 2003. http://www.pbs.org/thisfarbyfaith/people/henry_mcneal_turner.html (accessed 6 June 2007).

p. 82, par. 1, Redkey, *Black Exodus*, 196.

p. 82, par. 2, Redkey, *Black Exodus*, 237.

p. 82, par. 3, Redkey, *Black Exodus*, 293.

p. 84, par. 1, Booker T. Washington, "Atlanta Exposition Speech" (speech, Atlanta, GA, September 18, 1895). The Library of Congress American Memory, http://memory.loc.gov (accessed 12 June 2007).

p. 84, par. 3, Medley, *We as Freemen*, 190.

p. 85, par. 1, Mark Elliott, *Color-Blind Justice: Albion Tourgée and the Quest for Racial Equality* (Oxford, UK: Oxford University Press, 2006), 280.

Chapter 6

p. 88, par. 1, Maureen Hoch, "Supreme Court Watch: Terms and Traditions," The Online NewsHour, PBS, 2003. http://www.pbs.org/newshour/indepth_coverage/law/supreme_court/history_terms.html (accessed 27 June 2007).

Supreme Court Traditions

p. 89, par. 2, Richard Eadie, "Courting Fashion," King County Bar Association *Bulletin*, http://www.koba.org (accessed 27 June 2007).

p. 90, par. 3, Catherine Hetos Skefos, "The Supreme Court Gets a Home, Supreme Court Historical Society, 1975, http://www.supremecourthistory.org (accessed 27 June 2007).

p. 90, par. 4, Skefos, "The Supreme Court Gets a Home."

p. 91, par. 2, Steven G. Calabresi and James Lindgren, "Terms Limits for the Supreme Court: Life Tenure Reconsidered," *Harvard Journal of Law and Public Policy* (Summer 2006): 769.

p. 88, par. 3, Mark Elliott, *Color-Blind Justice: Albion Tourgée and the Quest for Racial Equality* (Oxford, UK: Oxford University Press, 2006), 282.

p. 88, par. 4, Otto H. Olsen, ed., *The Thin Disguise:* Plessy v. Ferguson, *A Documentary Presentation (1864–1896)* (New York: Humanities Press, 1967), 83.

p. 92, par. 2, Olsen, *The Thin Disguise*, 86.

p. 92, par. 4, Olsen, *The Thin Disguise*, 90.

p. 92, par. 4, Olsen, *The Thin Disguise*, 97.

p. 93, par. 1, Olsen, *The Thin Disguise*, 102, 103.

p. 93, par. 4, *Plessy* v. *Ferguson*, 163 U.S. 537 (1896),
http://curiae.law.yale.edu

p. 94, par. 1, *Plessy* v. *Ferguson*.

p. 94, par. 4, *Plessy* v. *Ferguson*.

p. 95, par. 3, Brook Thomas, ed., *Plessy v. Ferguson: A Brief History with Documents* (Boston: Bedford Books, 1997), 43.

p. 95, par. 4, Thomas, *Plessy v. Ferguson*, 44.

p. 96, par. 1, Thomas, *Plessy v. Ferguson*, 44.

p. 97, par. 2–4, Thomas, *Plessy v. Ferguson*, 50–51.

p. 98, par. 2, Thomas, *Plessy v. Ferguson*, 55.

p. 98, par. 4 and p. 102, par. 1–3, Thomas, *Plessy* v. *Ferguson*, 53–58.

The Great Dissenter

p. 99, par. 1, Linda Przybyszewski, "Afterword," *Some Memories of a Long Life, 1854–1911* by Malvina Shanklin Harlan. (New York: The Modern Library, 2002), 225.

p. 99, par. 1, Harlan, *Some Memories of a Long Life*, 21.

p. 99, par. 1, Harvey Fireside, *Separate and Unequal: Homer Plessy and the Supreme Court Decision that Legalized Racism* (New York: Carroll & Graf Publishers, 2004), 174.

p. 99, par. 1, Harlan, *Some Memories of a Long Life*, 113.

p. 99, par. 1, Lisa Paddock, PhD, LLB. *Supreme Court for Dummies* (New York: Wiley Publishing, Inc., 2002), 123.

p. 99, par. 1, "John Marshall Harlan." *American Eras, Volume 8: Development of the Industrial United States, 1878–1899.* Gale Research, 1997. http://galenet.galegroup.com/servlet/BioRC (accessed 15 June 2007).

p. 99, par. 1, Paddock, *Supreme Court for Dummies*, 121.

p. 99, par. 1, Tinsley E. Yarbrough, *Judicial Enigma: The First Justice Harlan* (New York: Oxford University Press), 229.

p. 103, par. 1, Thomas, *Plessy v. Ferguson*, 53–58.

Chapter 7

p. 105, par. 1, C. Vann Woodward. "The Case of the Louisiana Traveler" in *Quarrels that Have Shaped the Constitution*, ed. John A. Garraty. (New York: Harper & Row, Publishers, 1987), 172–173.

p. 105, par. 1, Otto H. Olsen, ed. *The Thin Disguise: Plessy v. Ferguson, A Documentary Presentation (1864–1896)* (New York: Humanities Press, 1967), 127.

p. 106, par. 1, Keith Weldon Medley, *We as Freemen: Plessy v. Ferguson* (Graetna, LA: Pelican Publishing, Co., 2003), 206.

p. 107, par. 1 and 3, Medley, *We as Freemen*, 218–221.

p. 108, par. 2, Medley, *We as Freemen*, 218–221.

p. 108, par. 4–p. 109, par. 1, Brook Thomas, ed., *Plessy v. Ferguson: A Brief History with Documents* (Boston: Bedford Books, 1997), 171.

p. 110, par. 1, Lisa Paddock, PhD, LLB. *Supreme Court for Dummies* (New York: Wiley Publishing, Inc., 2002), 230.

p. 110, par. 3, Medley, *We as Freemen*, 222.

p. 110, par. 7–p. 111, par. 1, Paddock, *Supreme Court for Dummies*, 231.

Mendez v. Westminster

p. 112, par. 3, Fermin Leal, "A Desegregation Landmark," *The Orange County Register* (March 21, 2007), http://www.mendezvwestminster.com/

p. 113, par. 1, University of Central Florida, "Woman Recalls Poor Treatment by White Students after Father's Lawsuit Integrated California Schools," news release by Mallery Laing, October 21, 2004. http://www.cah.ucf.edu/news/2004-Mendez.php

p. 113, par. 1, Laing, "Woman Recalls Poor Treatment."

p. 111, par. 3, Paddock, *Supreme Court for Dummies*, 234.

p. 111, par. 4, Harvey Fireside, *Separate and Unequal: Homer Plessy and the Supreme Court Decision that Legalized Racism* (New York: Carroll & Graf Publishers, 2004), 297.

p. 114, par. 1, Paddock, *Supreme Court for Dummies*, 234.

p. 115, par. 2, Thomas, Plessy *v.* Ferguson, 172.

p. 115, par. 3, Paddock, *Supreme Court for Dummies*, 237.

p. 116, par. 1, Michael J. Klarman, "*Brown* v. *Board* 50 Years Later," *Humanities* (March/April 2004) http://hnn.us/ articles/5097.html (accessed 16 July 2007).

p. 116, par. 2, Fireside, *Separate and Unequal*, 310.

p. 116, par. 3, "The *Adarand* Case: Affirmative Action and Equal Protection," Constitutional Rights Foundation, http://www.crf-usa.org/brown50th/adarand_affirmative_ action.htm (accessed 16 July 2007).

Thurgood Marshall

p. 118, par. 1–2, Thurgood Marshall, *Contemporary Heroes and Heroines, Book II* (Farmington Hills, MI: Thomson Gale, 1992). Also available online at http://galenet.galegroup. com/servlet/BioRC (accessed 6 July 2007).

p. 119, par. 1–4, Lisa Paddock, PhD, LLB, *Supreme Court for Dummies* (New York: Wiley Publishing, Inc., 2002), 236.

p. 117, par. 3, Adam Fairclough, *Better Day Coming: Blacks and Equality, 1890–2000* (New York: Viking, 2001), 329.

p. 117, par. 4, Richard Wolffe and Daren Briscoe, "Across the Divide," *Newsweek*, July 16, 2007, 26.

p. 120, par. 2–3, Linda Greenhouse, "Justices Limit the Use of Race in School Plans for Integration," *New York Times*, June 29, 2007. http://www.nytimes.com (accessed 29 June 2007).

p. 121, par. 1, Greenhouse, "Justices Limit the Use of Race in School Plans for Integration,"

p. 121, par. 2–p. 122, par. 1, "Excerpts from Opinions on the Use of Race in Public School Admission Policies," *New York Times*, June 29, 2007. http://www.nytimes.com (accessed 29 June 2007).

p. 122, par. 3, Thomas, Plessy *v.* Ferguson, 176.

FurTHer information

Books

Aaseng, Nathan. *Plessy v. Ferguson: Separate but Equal.* Farmington Hills, MI: Lucent Books, 2003.

Anderson, Wayne. *Plessy v. Ferguson: Legalizing Segregation.* New York: The Rosen Publishing Group, Inc., 2003.

Collier, Christopher and James Lincoln Collier. *Reconstruction and the Rise of Jim Crow, 1864–1896.* New York: Benchmark Books, 1999.

Sharp, Anne Wallace. *A Dream Deferred: The Jim Crow Era.* Farmington Hills, MI: Lucent Books, 2005.

Sirimarco, Elizabeth. *American Voices from the Civil Rights Movement.* New York: Benchmark Books, 2004.

Uschan, Michael V. *Lynching and Murder in the Deep South.* San Diego: Lucent Books, 2006.

Young, Mitchell, ed. *Racial Discrimination.* Farmington Hills, MI: Thomson Gale, 2006.

Web Sites

Brown v. Board of Education/Brown Foundation
http://brownvboard.org

The Curiae Project: United States Supreme Court Records and Briefs
http://curiae.law.yale.edu/

French Creoles of America
http://www.frenchcreoles.com

The History of Jim Crow
http://www.jimcrowhistory.org

Landmark Supreme Court Cases
http://www.landmarkcases.org

National Association for the Advancement of Colored
  People
http://www.naacp.org

Our Documents
http://ourdocuments.gov

Oyez—The Oyez Project
http://www.oyez.org

Supreme Court Historical Society
http://www.supremecourthistory.org

BIBLIOGraPHY

Books and Articles

Blassingame, John. W. *Black New Orleans: 1860–1880*. Chicago: The University of Chicago Press, 1973.

Carter, Hodding, ed. *The Past as Prelude; New Orleans 1718–1968*. New Orleans: Tulane University, 1968.

Elliott, Mark. *Color-Blind Justice: Albion Tourgée and the Quest for Racial Equality*. Oxford, UK: Oxford University Press, 2006.

"Excerpts from Opinions on the Use of Race in Public School Admission Policies," *New York Times*, June 29, 2007. http://www.nytimes.com

Fireside, Harvey. *Separate and Unequal: Homer Plessy and the Supreme Court Decision that Legalized Racism*. New York: Carroll & Graf Publishers, 2004.

Fischer, Roger A. *The Segregation Struggle in Louisiana: 1862–77*. Urbana: University of Illinois Press, 1974.

Klarman, Michael J. *From Jim Crow to Civil Rights: The Supreme Court and the Struggle for Racial Equality*. New York: Oxford University Press, 2004.

Klarman, Michael J. "The Plessy Era," *Supreme Court Review* (Annual 1998), 303.

Lofgren, Charles A. *The Plessy Case: A Legal-Historical Interpretation*. New York: Oxford University Press, 1987.

Medley, Keith Weldon. *We as Freemen: Plessy v. Ferguson*. Graetna, LA: Pelican Publishing Co., 2003.

Olsen, Otto H. *Carpetbagger's Crusade: The Life of Albion Winegar Tourgée.* Baltimore: The John Hopkins Press, 1965.

Olsen, Otto H. ed. *The Thin Disguise:* Plessy *v.* Ferguson. New York: Humanities Press, 1967.

Sharp, Anne Wallace. *A Dream Deferred: The Jim Crow Era.* Farmington Hills, MI: Lucent Books, 2005.

Welke, Barbara Young. *Recasting American Liberty: Gender, Race, Law, and the Railroad Revolution, 1865–1920.* Cambridge, UK: Cambridge University Press, 2001.

Woodward, C. Vann. *The Strange Career of Jim Crow.* New York: Oxford University Press, 1974.

Court Documents

Brown v. *Board of Education of Topeka,* 347 U.S. 483 (1954).

Civil Rights Cases, 109 U.S. 3 (1883).

Hall v. *DeCuir,* 95 U.S. 485 (1878).

Louisville, New Orleans and Texas Railway Company v. *Mississippi,* 133 U.S. 587 (1890).

Parents Involved in Community Schools v. *Seattle School District,* 551 U.S. __ (2007).

Plessy v. *Ferguson,* 163 U.S. 537 (1896).

Regents of the University of California v. *Bakke,* 438 U.S. 265 (1978).

Slaughterhouse Cases, 83 U.S. 36 (1873).

Strauder v. *West Virginia,* 100 U.S. 303, (1880).

U.S. v. *Cruikshank,* 92 U.S. 542 (1876).

West Chester and Philadelphia Railroad Company v. *Miles,* 55 Pa. 209 (1867).

Yick Wo v. *Hopkins,* 188 U.S. 356 (1886).

index

Page numbers in **boldface** are illustrations, tables, and charts.

ABOUT THE AUTHOR

Joan Axelrod-Contrada is the author of several books for middle-school and high-school students. She has written about a variety of topics, including women leaders, the Lizzie Borden trial, colonial America, and the soccer player Mia Hamm. Her most recent book for Marshall Cavendish is titled *Drug Abuse and Society*. The author's work has also appeared in the *Boston Globe* and various other publications, including *Writer's Digest*. In addition, she teaches a freelance writing course at the University of Massachusetts at Amherst.